BEFORE YOU WERE YOU

THE METAMORPHOSIS OF A SOUL

KATHRYN GRANT

BALBOA.
PRESS

A DIVISION OF HAY HOUSE

Balboa Press books may be ordered through booksellers or by contacting:

Balboa Press
A Division of Hay House
1663 Liberty Drive
Bloomington, IN 47403
www.balboapress.com
1 (877) 407-4847

Because of the dynamic nature of the Internet, any web addresses or links contained in this book may have changed since publication and may no longer be valid. The views expressed in this work are solely those of the author and do not necessarily reflect the views of the publisher, and the publisher hereby disclaims any responsibility for them.

The author of this book does not dispense medical advice or prescribe the use of any technique as a form of treatment for physical, emotional, or medical problems without the advice of a physician, either directly or indirectly. The intent of the author is only to offer information of a general nature to help you in your quest for emotional and spiritual well-being. In the event you use any of the information in this book for yourself, which is your constitutional right, the author and the publisher assume no responsibility for your actions.

Any people depicted in stock imagery provided by Thinkstock are models, and such images are being used for illustrative purposes only.
Certain stock imagery © Thinkstock.

Print information available on the last page.

ISBN: 978-1-5043-7310-4 (sc)
ISBN: 978-1-5043-7311-1 (hc)
ISBN: 978-1-5043-7322-7 (e)

Library of Congress Control Number: 2017900583

Balboa Press rev. date: 03/09/2017

CONTENTS

DEDICATIONS & GRATEFULNESS

This book is dedicated to the five amazing, beautifully delicious creations I am privileged to call my children. Taylor, Hillary, Ashton, Tristan & Kieran. You have imprinted on my soul and we are forever together, now as we were in the creation realm. You have brought more love and light into my life than I deserve.

For Roger. You opened your heart and soul and offered me and my family comfort, strength, stability, a new perspective, a second chance and a love I never knew I was worthy of. Soul mates forever. I've known you for a thousand years. We will never truly say farewell, bound by the heart, connected at the soul level. Thank you for pushing me ever so lovingly toward this accomplishment. I am eternally grateful.

For Robin and Wayne, who truly are angels that walk among us. I love you and will never in a million lifetimes be able to thank you for your generosity, love, support and the safety net of comfort and peace you provided me and my family as we traveled down an uncharted road of loss, grief, and survival. You are amazing friends and will forever be in our hearts and minds with love, gratitude, and prayers for your prosperity, health and well- being forever and ever.

A special thank you to Wendy, Julie, and Laurie who took the time to read the thoughts within my heart and had the courage to tell me what I needed to hear.

For Mother. You not only gave me life but also taught me faith, love, kindness and perseverance.

For KC Miller who encouraged me to write my story and through a generous heart, held out the hand of hope as I journeyed into becoming a life coach.

For Abel, Arrow, Lucy, Emerson, Isla, and Mila … "Fear not, for I am with you says the Lord." Be fearless in your dreaming, relentless in your pursuit of goodness, and intentional in your creating the life you can see clearly in your imagination. Remember that "Honey" will always love you.

In memory of my late husband Rick, for giving me 34 years of love and life, and encouraging me to write my truth. You're the bravest person I've ever known. I will never stop missing you…until we meet again.

INTRODUCTION

Somewhere deep inside all of us is a calling, a small soft voice that says "I'm here! Now what?" But where is "here?" And where was I in the first place? My name is Kathryn Grant, but everyone calls me Kate. I am a fellow human being with all of the responsibilities that come with family, friendships, romantic relationships, business obligations and the rest of the pressures that life serves up to us on a not so silver platter. I am overworked, underpaid, tired, frustrated, elated, excited and challenged. However, equally inspired and hopeful that this world will someday raise its consciousness to a place where it all makes sense. A world where every human life is valued and humans feel a part of a collective whole. A place where we can be *a part of*, not *apart from* something greater than ourselves, our own needs, our silly insecurities, our lack of focus on what's true and right and divine.

I'm a no frills, fifty-something southern girl with all the spit and vinegar that comes with growing up with five brothers. I wear boots and shorts, and my favorite casual food is a good burger and a beer. But put me in front of an awesome steak and seafood dinner in a little black dress and I can work every fork on the table. Just add wine. I grew up with cotillion, and debutants, rode horses, attended dance classes, and went to church. I was scared to death of the tornadoes that had us hiding inside the bathtub, and spent summers swatting mosquitos, watching for rattle snakes, and shucking fresh corn with my Grandmother on the patio. What's there not to enjoy about all the magnificent tastes, sounds, sights, smells, and touches of this unbelievable place I call the physical realm? Being an entrepreneur for 35 years, I've had my share of successes and failures, and I'm still here. I've owned retail stores and manufacturing businesses, dance studios and other small ventures. But my greatest accomplishment is standing in the humility of myself. My truth. Accepting who I am for what I am, and giving myself the grace to screw up and look ridiculous for trying and failing.

My family is by far my paramount achievement, yet not of my doing, but of God's grace. I have always made it my intention to love and care for my five children like the treasures that they are. Like special gifts from heaven meant only for me and their father. They have taught me more about the loving intentional creation that we all are than any other experience except for one. You see ... I've carried a secret with me an entire lifetime. An experience that needs to be shared with my fellow human beings in an effort to inspire someone, somewhere, and leave a small contribution to the world. To throw my arms around the human race and squeeze tightly with the warmth that only we can bestow on each other while in our physical bodies. I have been given a gift from beyond. I have kept it a secret all of these years, until now. I'm ready to whisper it within these pages.

We are spirits all of us, encased in a beautiful expression of what the Creator intended us to be. Threads in a tapestry that is ever changing its gorgeous appearance as we each weave our story into the divine fabric of creation. We are all a part of this gorgeous, intentional expression. We are each an amazing piece of this beautiful spec of history. We are all truly connected.

Being a widow has been everything I feared and more. I hate that word. It's so dark and even when we speak it, there is an ugly distortion to our mouths. It's like a sentence to forever be sorrowful, lonely, and depressed. A life sentence without parole. I am but a broken hearted remnant of a 31 year marriage to a once high school sweetheart that I grew up with and wanted to grow old with. The mother of five exquisite creatures that are the most amazing gifts to my unworthy soul. And when my grandchildren call me "Honey" it's the sweetest sound I've yet to hear uttered above all the delightful music in the world. Being a widow, according to our society, one is supposed to be disappointed, jaded, embittered, angry, and forlorn.

Yet I am happy, I am an innocent soul that was shattered, then prodded by faith and courage to keep going, move forward into a life I had only imagined once before. My secret must be told. It's time to encourage others to make their mark. Allow themselves to journey back to the beginning and find the part of themselves that is lost, lonely, unloved, frustrated, ignored, patronized, bullied or otherwise downtrodden because of the bitter pill that life has somehow prescribed them; and use that experience to push through, evolve, learn to love from the heart and by doing so, reveal the radiance that only comes from the soul engaged, ignited and hopeful, only daring to rise above the mediocrity that most humans call this life. Not just existing but thriving!

It can be done. It's not a pill, a twelve step plan or a "get awesome quick" scheme. It's a mirror and some courage to "play chicken" with the reflected image. It is facing the truth about who we are and where we came from. It's about reaching the inner self and falling in love with it. Remembering where we came from and the true nature of ourselves as human beings.

I'm a friend, daughter, mother, grandmother, wife, sister, and independent woman. I'm an entrepreneur, a dancer, a life coach, an author, and live a holistic lifestyle. My story is riddled with familiarity for some and for others just a peek into a world of someone who's experience has touched them in such a way as to change the world she lived in. Once I stood in the truth of myself, I was able to just "be." I became more forgiving, more loving; a genuine soul that attracted and exuded light and love, understanding, and grace. My life became a flowing easy road rather than a steep uphill grind.

This is my truth. This is my gift. This is the story of all of us.

BEFORE YOU WERE YOU

Your true self. Your innate, organic, awesome, awe-inspiring, amazing self yearns for a deeper sense of purpose. Why are we here? Why is life so difficult? Why do we feel stuck?

We were created to be that which we are. Beauty, joy, bliss, thinkers, Creators, confident, hopeful, happy, funny, active.

We are loved just by "being." We are approved of just by living.

We are the Creator's most beautiful expression of himself.

We are limitless

We are intended

We are purposeful

We are powerful

We are boundless

We are endless

We are eternal …

We are embraced by the entire scope of creation.

All of everything loves us.

This is where we came from.

This is who we are meant to be.

"My soul is from elsewhere, I'm sure of that, and I intend to end up there."

– <u>Rumi</u>

We are limited in this physical form to its laws, but our spirits strive to find a place of peace. A place without resistance through contemplation and meditation. Our spirits yearn to find their organic place of rest so that our entire being can be at peace with this world and our eternal place. Only here in this place of knowing can we fully express what we were created to be.

When we deny the existence of GOD, source-energy, universal power, the Creator … eternity … pure divine loving energy … we deny ourselves … that of which we ARE.

Our physical mind holds only a limited understanding of this concept, however the spirit knows … our spirit always knows … and some of us remember …

CHAPTER 1

BEING HUMAN

As humans, we tend to believe what we are taught. We are innately curious from birth, observing and recording everything we see, touch, hear, taste, and smell. Our brains have an enormous capacity for learning. We form our thoughts and even base most of our emotions on what has been communicated to us through loving, well-meaning parents, teachers, friends, siblings, and extended family. The planet itself even programs our events and experiences through weather patterns, the rhythms of the ocean waves, the moon cycles, and the rotations around the sun that define our cycles of activities and sleep patterns. All of these outside influences are integral parts of our human experience.

This has been one of the most challenging hurdles for me on this journey of believing and sharing. Just encouraging others to actually embrace the possibility that this truly was our experience and that we all are intrinsically destined, designed uniquely to participate in a dance that was choreographed before the beginning of time. I myself have even found it difficult to believe from time to time. You would think that remembering this experience would give me a bolder sense of myself, and although I do possess an abundance of faith and what I would describe as a super-weird sense of "Everything is going to be okay and I'm exactly where I'm supposed to be; it has all been worked out for me," I'm a human. I get depressed, feel defeated, get confused, am frustrated—a lot—and experience the entire scope of human emotions that we all feel. I wish I were some sort of superhuman who was an all-knowing, all-loving being who wore an awesome cape that seemed to flow even when there wasn't any breeze. I wish I could scale tall buildings in a single bound, although that would just be showing off! And who wouldn't want to rescue all the puppies in the world, superhero style? But I am human. I am frail. I get scared. I hesitate. I make mistakes—a lot of them! So I am not a perfect human who has "all of this" figured out. Just because I have been given a rare gift of remembering what the "where" was like before I was born, it doesn't mean I have a different path from other humans. We are all connected. We all have to and get to experience this beautiful, tragic, emotional, intensely challenging physical life together.

I am not perfect, for sure. But I do have fun! I dance when no one is watching and equally in the car with music booming in front of everyone. I love to get wet in the rain and act like it isn't messing up my hair, because no one in the state of Colorado owns an umbrella. And when I fall down, I immediately look around to see who saw me because if a tree falls in the woods and no one hears it?

I love deeply, intentionally, and naively. I say stupid things without thinking. I praise the accomplishments of others because I truly love the light of their existence and wish we could all share the vision of when we were created and didn't struggle so much with ourselves. I also in the past have looked for a superhuman idol who could make my life better with a system, a pill or even an e-book, like many of us. All you will find in these pages is truth told from a genuine heart that let its defenses down long enough to spew forth a secret that has been haunting it for five decades.

I didn't ask for this experience that I'm about to share. From as far back as I can remember, and even before, apparently, I knew I was different. I knew that the things I thought about, recalled, and was drawn to made me different. Weird. And it scared me. As a child of four or five years old, I would lie in bed, put myself into a deep trance, and go back for and reexperience everything I'd seen and remembered. Every night. I would lie in my bed, closing my eyes tightly, and force myself to clear my mind. When a thought popped into my brain, I would quickly take deep breaths and focus on the vision of "the others."

I wasn't sure at the time how I could possibly remember or what I was even experiencing, but I knew I was drawn to it. Like a drug that transcends the pain of the flesh into a painless, carefree, effortless existence, I was taken willingly into this place, and it was irresistible. My days were spent deep in thought. The other kids were playing, and I knew I wanted to play too. They never chose me for the team first. I was always a last choice. Withdrawn with a serious nature, I was also a very happy and carefree child: a strange mix for making and keeping friends. I could make friends all right, but the moment I began to speak of "the others" or tell them about my wonderful "dreams," they would withdraw my rights of friendship and label me as the weird kid. I wanted to fit in. I wanted to be the girl others thought was pretty, but I wasn't. I wanted to be the girl whose mother worked in the classroom to help the teacher, but I wasn't. I wished for my hair to be beautifully braided with a ribbon that matched our green and blue plaid uniforms—you know those classic Catholic schoolgirl uniforms—but it wasn't. I knew that I was apart from the other human beings who surrounded me. I daydreamed of the beautiful light beings, the "others" who loved me, and I tried to remember what that was like. This world was loud and had rules. It was more difficult to be who I knew inside that I truly was: this beautiful light being without limits. I yearned to be back with the others. I cried at times because I was here on earth and desired greatly the opportunity to be back again where I felt I belonged. Sometimes even now, I realize that I don't belong here. Then I wrap my mind around the idea that this is a temporary space. That it is a privilege to become flesh and experience the beauty of the human race in this form. It is purposeful, meaningful, and lovely yet can sometimes be harsh, unkind, unfair, and brutally painful.

This world is mundane compared with the creation realm. Even with the beauty of nature in all of its glory and majesty and those manmade things that were thrust from the imaginations of the brilliant. This world has its own interpretation of beauty, but nothing compares to the infinite beauty that is felt in the place we were created. It is all-encompassing love, and every creation shares a purity of spirit. That is where we came from and where we return to on some level when we are gone from here. It is just one dream that fades into another dream. Life is but a dream, but don't just row! Live, love, grow, expand, and experience this physical realm as part of the beauty of existence itself. Remember that we are all in a temporary place and time here moves more slowly than in that realm, where time doesn't exist as we know it. Our lives here are but a vapor, and then we are released back into our spirit form.

I was seventh out of eight kids in a big Catholic family with some social standing. My parents worked hard for their success and were highly thought of in our community. They were business owners and well known, but not social in a socialite sort of way. They were extremely dedicated to our faith and church. All of the children attended Catholic school, and they were big supporters. I remember growing up proud of my family and proud of our name. It brought me vicarious pride to drive up to the family business and see my last name on a sign and on invoices with people who were happy to do business with us.

My dad was a hardworking man and never felt that what success he had accomplished was anything he deserved. He was humble and contrite of heart. He was strong and yet relied on my mother's strength and direction. He was a handsome man in a Jimmy Stewart sort of way, and I always thought he was attractive and his inner light shined so brightly that he was charismatic. Anyone who ever met Johnny walked away with a sense of gratefulness to have made his acquaintance. He was the type of man that other men wanted to be: honest, strong, sensitive, smart, hardworking, and dedicated to his family. God, he loved his family.

My fondest memories of my dad were sitting on his lap on Sunday afternoons and watching the Dallas Cowboys play during their heyday—before all of the wife beatings and drugs. This is when professional athletes were made of grit and brawn and integrity and weren't out for the spotlight. They weren't trying to marry Hollywood and were grateful for their success instead of abusing it like so many do now. These were the days of Roger Staubach, Walt Garrison, and Drew Pearson. I remember the smell of Dad's gourd pipe as he cleaned it out and set it on the table next to his recliner. As I cuddled in his lap and named each player by jersey number and position, I never felt more loved or more important to anyone—ever. I asked my mother for that pipe after he passed and she willingly gave it to me. I still press it close to my face and close my eyes and am taken back to that place of comfort, love, and acceptance. I was my Daddy's little girl and he always loved me. His bold, loving, friendly nature has been my inheritance. I remember his words of wisdom about how to treat others and his work ethic. I've always prided myself on being a hard worker.

However, I always knew I was different. Something just wasn't right about me. It wasn't until I was much older that I actually realized how different I was ... how different I am. Let us begin this journey together.

It is my heartfelt desire to transcribe into words these ethereal experiences that are mine alone. This is my gift from God. My blessing to the world. It was not asked for, it was given. I did not want this but was chosen for it. I never thought it my intention to become an author, speaker, or messenger, and yet I cannot escape it. It has become my intention, my purpose, and passion.

This shared experience is from a private place of love, peace, understanding, and bliss. It is eternal. It is special. It is for everyone, yet I know not everyone will receive it. There is a sadness in this for me that all souls need to hear the message of inspiration and peace, yet some choose their own limited intelligence over what has been freely given by our Creator. This is a journey back to self. It is a journey back to truth. I wish for this not to be some senseless persuasion but instead, present a truthful account of my experience, not an egotistically tainted version of the truth. My very name means pure and so I endeavor to manifest this into its purest form and somehow touch the lives of others through my experience. We are all divinely created with a specific purpose to which many of us will never aspire to become. We get lost, caught up somehow in the day to day-ness of our lives. The potentiality of each carefully designed and designated human being is so very great ... infinite in so many aspects. It is my deepest desire to communicate this to every human being on the planet so that while we are here in this physical plane, we can become fully the expression that we were intended to be. By embracing and acknowledging that we are each and individually meant to be ... set in motion by the Creator of all ... we can accomplish and become even more than we ever thought possible. By tapping into the universal knowledge that we are each ordained specifically by the Creator of the universe, we find not only ourselves but our connection to others, our world, and the universe. In denying this connection, we separate ourselves from the very thing that we are. Human yet infinite. Limited yet limitless.

My soul's purpose is to be careful not careless in delivering this message. Fearless, not fearful in taking this gift and no longer hoarding it for myself or being fearful of what the outcome will be, but allowing it to be shared. I am again a little girl, frightened of what others might think of me. I am timid and know that I am different. I am a quiet observer of others and know I do not fit in, yet I am inspired, pushed, relentlessly prompted to deliver it, without regard to consequences of it. It is time.

CHAPTER 2

THE BEGINNING

Let us begin at the beginning …

It is my sincerest wish that others could see themselves as God sees them … the brightest light. A reflection of (himself) … radiant, beautiful, pure … magnificent. A perfect reflection of all that is good, with nothing lacking or wanton.

> *"And when we harness the inner light and beauty of our soul within, we are the most powerful, creative, successful, loving version of ourselves and that brings us the inner peace we are all searching for."*-Kate

The lesson is this. We are a part of our God … our Creator and He is in us. That is a truth that is not altered because of our bag of flesh we recognize as our bodies. We are not hindered by this time and space to be who we truly are, and who we are created to be. Our spirits are alive and never die. The spirit is the essence of who we are, captured inside these thirty-seven trillion cells that contain it, but not defined by it, nor is it truly the sum of ourselves. The soul is not fat or bald, it does not have limitations of mobility or sight, it does not get cancer, stupid fucking cancer. It doesn't age and is not hindered by deformity. It certainly does not define itself by how it makes its' living. The soul shines brightly and is not limited because of saggy breasts, wrinkles, arthritis, irritable bowel, warts, skin conditions, genetic disorder, arthritis, gluten intolerance, nor male or female orientation. Its' light cannot be dimmed by the judgment of others, the idea that the "world" has formulated about it or the insignificance of wealth, power, accomplishment, social status, or lack thereof.

The soul's light burns brightly and purely even when we are asleep. It is always who we are. It is our power, our true selves, the one truth. We are never without it. The alluring creations of this world may entrap us for a little while, but in the end … truly in the end of this physical existence when the soul leaves the body, we are set free and understand that this was only an experience. One of many. We were here to burn brightly and then not burn out but shine in a different place, in a different dimension, in a different way. Our bodies are not so separate from us that they are unimportant. We are formed in the beauty of the human likeness of our

Creator, and it is a profound misunderstanding that we somehow use them up and then discard them, however it was not my experience in the creation realm when I first came to be and understand, that I had a body. I was not a body, only pure light and intelligence … a consciousness. I was only my soul. When I was shown my life, I then completely recognized that I was a human and I knew which one. I saw myself for the first time. I believe that our flesh is divinely crafted as well. Our physical appearance in its' entirety; the way that we look, the way we are built, our physical attributes and capabilities, and the color of our skin, hair and eyes, all play integral parts in our existence here on earth and that is something that cannot be disregarded when speaking of the whole person. Body, mind, spirit. We are not only mind and spirit but our bodies are ultimately what give us the ability to experience this expression and so we should really take care of our bodies! What a privilege to be human. What an awesomely exhilarating experience to have a body that we can grow into, move around in and accomplish and experience so much here. The taste of a juicy peach, or the tartness of a lemon, that smell of vanilla in the sugar cookies fresh out of the oven. Let's not forget those pumpkin spice "everythings" that pop up once a year in the harvest season. The feeling of a tender kiss or the beauty of a sunset. The sound of your favorite song when you haven't heard it in a long while, how the harmonies bring back soulful memories. My life would never be the same without having heard my lover's voice softly whisper "I love you, and waking up with you is my favorite thing."

Ultimately the one truth is that we are created by He who has no beginning and no end. Our minds cannot comprehend this and so we seek to understand and our egos are not satiated by the answers we invent to make ourselves feel quieted and pacified.

We are created as beautiful, unique mirrored reflections of the one true LOVE, nothing lacking, nothing negative, only passionate joy, love, bliss, peace ... and when we are set before him, he is delighted with us. He imbued us with His beautiful essence and is so very pleased. We must strive then, to brighten our light and shine it from within. Using gratitude, grace, love, and kindness in our vocabulary of living. Setting our sights on being the beautiful creations we were always meant to be and allowing our souls to shine through the darkness of this world and spread the light of our inner selves to others. SHINE on ... because you truly are still the creation you were ...

Before You were YOU.

What then is the importance of this experience? What is the real reason we are here? What are humans anyway? I began to ponder these questions as such a young child, even as young as three or four. I wondered ... I know that we are people and that people live in the world ...

on the earth and that there are solar systems etc ... but what ARE we? In eternity ... what are humans and what is outside of the human existence? A darkness? Only a black cold space? And if we are consciousness then who is observing us? What else is out there looking at us and what is our purpose? These questions were too much for my mind to comprehend or reason out so I began meditating back to a place where it didn't matter. The soul knows what the soul knows. It isn't lacking and there are no disturbing questions. Within the space and time that I was when I first "began" there were no unanswered questions. There was nothing to question at all. I was an intelligence that simply "knew." I was at peace with everything around me and never cared about such ponderings.

I simply WAS.

The significance of this experience is that we are destined. We are ordained ... we are meant to be. The theories that have been placed before us about our just being an organic mass of flesh that has somehow crawled up from pond scum are not only inherently inaccurate but also preposterous to those of us who have had divine experiences here on earth. Those of us that live an intuitive life seeing the divine light of creation in almost every experience consider these pond scum theories as the musings of the insane. The lost. The hopeless. There is a lack of peace and an importance of self -intellect that is implied by those who somehow feel the need to ignore, challenge, and negate the idea that we are divinely inspired, created, and purposefully intended to be exactly who we are with distinct DNA, emotions, feelings, innate abilities, traits, and other fingerprints of God himself. However, those who are not in harmony with the idea of a Creator are fulfilling their purpose here in this physical realm as well. They are loved, adored, cherished, and treasured beyond measure, just like the seekers. The Creator adores all of his creations ... there is no trash. No one is wasted.

Before you were you ... you were a spark, an idea in the Creator's thoughts ... a dream, a hope, an inspired feeling of potential.

So here goes. It's like jumping off the ledge of the knowledgeable into a sea of uncertainty and speculation. This is the tale of the lifelong journey that has brought me to this point. I hope it is not taken lightly but could easily be brushed off as the musings of a hopeless romantic or misconstrued as a word from the wise. I am both romantic and wise. I am not, however, hopeless.

CHAPTER 3

THE CREATION REALM

As if someone turned on a switch ... I was "there".

Alive.

Aware.

But just before that I had a sense of being thrust, an energetic "push."

I was then able to observe things ... "see". I did not have a body as we know it ... only form. As I looked at where /who/what I came from, I was instantly delighted and in a state of sheer reverence and awe. I felt my soul "smiling." My being was filled with an ineffable sense of love, peace, purity, strength, knowing, and ecstasy that I've only experienced a shred of again at the first look into the eyes of my newborn children. Total freedom ... from what? I didn't even know yet ... but it was total freedom ... no pain, no worries ... nothing. Just a sense of "rightness."

When I looked upon that "thing" that I came from ...

It wasn't a person in the sense of physicality. There was no face or features … only a huge sphere of "light" with no exact edges or boundaries. Light was sort of bubbling out of it like lava so it was constant but ever changing.

I was captivated by the beauty of it and I knew this was my Creator.

I was keenly aware that I looked just like it. I was the exact same only much smaller and without the capacity to divide myself. I was whole, complete, lacking nothing … perfect.

There was absolutely no realization of time or space. The next experience in my awareness was that I wasn't alone. I became aware that there were others around me and I was delighted and instantly curious about them.

It was dark but not without light. It was an odd sense of "Where am I?" but knowing exactly where I was. I was the light.

There was no speaking … only understanding, yet there was sound. I heard muffled sounds as if there were a hundred radio stations playing all at the same time, but it wasn't chaotic. It was as if I could tune into any one specifically whenever I wanted to. If I heard a sound and was delighted by it, all I needed to do was focus for an instant and that was all I could hear. And the beauty of the "music" enveloped me. I was in it and it was in me.

There was no thinking … only a pure sense of being. I just ***was***.

I was potential, yet I was already fulfilled and perfect.

I had no thoughts of future, and none of past. I was only NOW. There was such a sense of the present moment that I was powerful yet needed no power. I was one with the Creator a separate being, but still connected to the Creator. There was no space between us, yet I knew He was more. There was no "bad" … Bad did not exist … only good. There was no hate … only love. The love did not exist to define the hate … love was love. It was everywhere. It permeated my being and the other beings. It was the very space that we were all "in." The place we occupied. It was blissful—ineffable—unadulterated **LOVE**. The deepest, warmest, most sincere, most organic, inherent **LOVE**. Total weightless, bliss.

There were others around me feeling joy. I could feel their joy. It permeated my being, and I could feel their love for me as well. "They" were in awe of me. It was bliss …

I was aware that I was once part of the Creator Himself, but now I had somehow become separate. I was aware that I was a special piece of HIM that was thrust into the universe to "become." Potential … an expression of love in its finest form.

It was similar to the moment that the moon no longer dominates the sky but the sun is not yet shining. There is light and you realize that something has changed in a profound way, because there is the acknowledgement that it is no longer night, and the daylight is present but not dominant. It is there in that very moment of early dawn, the dawn of my own creation, that I realized my possibility. I WAS possibility … potential, perfection.

It was mysterious and yet I felt I was exactly where I was supposed to be. I was communicating with someone or something, a being who was familiar. I knew Him and He knew me. I knew He was all knowing and safe. There was never a question of Him being my origin.

When I say this place that I "was" did not radiate light, I mean it was more like being in a huge black space with brilliant lights surrounding you … like millions of stars in a never ending sky. When the "stars" energy communicated with mine, I saw only their beauty. I was never afraid. This is where I belonged. It was comfortable and familiar even though I felt like I had just awakened into it for the first time.

Just imagine yourself with no limits … nothing tethered … totally free. No fear. Only pure acceptance, confidence, blissful creativity, joy, love, peace, freedom.

Any idea, thought, or notion can be instantly satisfied without effort.

That is who we truly are. Even in this world, that is who we truly are. The only thing holding us back is our own idea that we are not what we were created to be. The thoughts and influences of others and the world around us binds us to that idea, confining us as a caged bird with the urge to be set free, to soar above the ordinary and create and live in a world that is extraordinary. The limited ideology of a dated society formed out of the assumption that humans need to be controlled or we wouldn't have the social conscience to make order out of chaos is a notion that should no longer be embraced.

Brave, enlightened souls need to come forth ... the brazen, the bold, the independent thinkers who wish to create a new world that cares for the needs of others, because we are all connected. We need to imagine and create a future of peace and prosperity for all humans, and out of love, not greed, develop a system of a beautiful existence, not just for the wealthy or privileged, but for every human being on the planet, because we are all connected deeply from creation, rooted in the past of our past, even before we were born.

My time in the creation realm may have been brief and it could have been 100 years. There was not time or space. Those limitations did not exist.

The "others" were like fireflies on a summer's night floating carelessly through the midnight sky. Some of their lights burned brighter than others and I was curiously interested and being drawn nearer to them. They were beautiful and radiated pure, ineffable love. I have experienced love here as a human, but this love is indescribably different. It was/is pure ecstasy. So powerful that it would be overwhelming to us if we were to experience it here with our human hearts and understanding. The love was so pure, unadulterated, and beautiful that it actually enveloped me as if I entered some sort of gravitational pull into the other "being" and became a part of their light, their beauty. As I intertwined my soul with theirs, it became a dance of joy and bliss. It was as if I knew them and had been somehow separated from them and reunited in some way. When I "entered" their spirit, the focus became on their beauty and nothing else existed. I was never distracted by the beauty or movement of others when I was in this unity with each particular soul ... one at a time. Time, if there was such a thing in this realm, did not exist, it literally stopped. The only existence of anything at that exact moment was the "other" and myself, and yet we were one, separated by nothing ... completely united and fused into one another.

This union of light and love could have lasted only a moment or it could have been 1000 years, I don't know. I only know that it was the most exquisite experience I had in this realm apart from the complete ecstasy of the Creator and I reflecting each other's love, adoration, acceptance, and delight for each other after my first memory of self- actualization.

After this union with the "other" it felt as if there was a gain in momentum, some kind of inertia that led me from one being to the next, absorbing the beauty of each of the souls I intertwined with and leaving their beauty glowing a bit brighter myself as if I was being given a piece of their essence and leaving a bit of my own without either one of us losing anything. The closest thing I can compare it to is a mother's love for her children. Each of them has a piece of her heart, yet her heart grows bigger with the creation of each child. They both "grew." This is how it is in the creation realm. You contribute and by giving of yourself, you gain. Never lacking anything.

True confidence comes from knowing that we are all divinely created and physically here for a short time to love, observe and experience, and then we return to a non-physical/spiritual plane. Living our physical lives with this in mind, we are able to love deeper, connect more, worry less and have more fun here on this planet!

CHAPTER 4

GIVING TO RECEIVE

By giving you receive, and by allowing yourself to receive, you give.

The beauty of this experience has affected me my entire life in both my personal and professional relationships. By allowing myself to realize even here on earth that there is no need to hold back love, kindness, friendship, empathy, gratitude, blessing, belongings, money, joy, tears, advice, or anything else that is asked of us, it has changed the way that I see myself and others. I can be free to express and give anything I want to at any given time. I have focused on giving without fear, because when connected to the Creator, nothing is being taken from me that I won't receive back, tenfold or even more. I'd like to interject here that I am not perfect or in some way canonizing myself as a saint. I am broken, disillusioned, imperfect for sure, however I meditate on the goodness of others and how their specific talents and gifts, divinely inspired by the Creator Himself do not

23

hinder mine, nor somehow diminish my own divinely given talents and gifts, therefore they are not a threat to me.

When a friend of mine was going into business for herself, she asked if I would be willing to mentor her and share the pitfalls and successes of my own business with her. She had never started a business before and was bold enough to ask if I would help her. I was in no way threatened even though her business model was the same as mine and within 10 miles of my own shop. I was never once hesitant to help her, meet with her, and give her both my time and advice about how to avoid some of the mistakes I had experienced to save her time, effort, and money. By not holding back out of fear that she would somehow get ahead of me in business, I have had the privilege of watching both of our businesses flourish while others around us failed. This is a direct result of my experience in the creation realm where I was blessed with the opportunity to see how our souls benefit only when we let go and embrace the beauty and majesty of others. I have never once given of myself and/or my resources that they haven't been returned to me in excess of what was given. By giving what little we may have, we are returned a greater gift. Hearts bigger, souls shining more brightly … the way we were created to be. Just like it was in the creation realm where I entered the soul of another, absorbed their radiance and left some of mine neither of us lacking from the experience.

"The purpose of our creation in and of itself is to radiate light, and love. It is to be shared, enjoyed, delighted in and preserved. Brought into our true consciousness and lived fully while in this physical realm. Each and every day. Just relax into your life ... there is no "rat race" unless you truly are a rat."-Kate

CHAPTER 5

THE ESSENCE OF THE CREATOR

Before I was me, I WAS. Before we can fully understand who we are, or who we were, in this case, we must first look at where we came from. The Source, the Creator, the Universe, Universal knowledge, Source Energy, God, Jehovah, Elohim, Yahweh, are all labels man has created in order to understand that from which we came. It doesn't matter what you call Him/Her/It ... the Creator ... He simply is/was/always will be the source from which we came. It has always been curious to me that people will fight literally to the death over their religious beliefs rather than being quiet and listening to the sound of the soul that tells us we are all a part of the same design. We are all pursuing the same end. A deep relationship with what is inside of us. We all pursue a deeper understanding of who we are and why we are here. Something bigger than us. And standing in awe of its power, grace, mercy, and mystery, while experiencing the comfort of knowing that the power of this Creator is ever near, inside of us, always wanting our highest good. **New Heart English Bible**

> *God said to Moses, "I AM THAT I AM,"*
> *and he said, "You shall tell the children*
> *of Israel this: 'I AM has sent me to you.'*

After deep contemplation of the passage in the Bible that relates to God trying to expose himself to Moses, there was a pause in his verbiage. You know when you get a text and it all runs together because the person who sent it doesn't punctuate? Then you have to figure out what they were saying by reading it several times.

It has always been curious to me that possibly God needed a comma or semi-colon or even a hyphen. What I believe He said to Moses when asked "What is your name?" He said …" I am that," … "I am." "That" is defined as "Referring to a specific thing previously mentioned, known or understood." Breathing the words "I am" then "referring to a specific thing previously mentioned, known or understood." … "I am."

He simply was saying I "be" … I "exist" … I AM.

"Am" is defined as "1st person singular present of be."

"Be" is defined as "exist."

So God was saying to Moses "I simply AM." "I exist." "I simply exist."

Maybe He was saying "I'm not a what, a He, or a who." I am pure consciousness.

This was my experience in the creation realm. "He" is simply a term I have to use because of the limitations of our human language. The Creator was not male or female. There was no evidence of sexual definition. So as not to refer to the Creator as an "it," and because our human nature is to designate He or She … I will simply refer to this entity … our Creator as "He". When you read, feel free to substitute whatever makes your experience true for you. I don't wish to provoke anyone here, however we are uniquely and divinely created and all of us have our own programming that we are working with, so for simplicity sake and to deliver a more universally accepted message … "He" is what I chose.

He, she, God, the universe etc. It is not my intention to offend your beliefs or offer a religious examination of this experience but share what I believe was all of our experience for every person walking the earth at the present time and every soul that has come before us and is to come.

We were somewhere else. It was a place. I was aware of it. The Creator was light against the darkness.

These things I know …

The Creator is neither male nor female but an essence of both.

In our simplest form, we are bright clear light/energy/consciousness.

There is no physical sense of feeling … hot or cold.

Space was infinitely around us.

We radiated "ourselves" into each other in a beautiful exchange of energy.

The light within "us" is the divine light of our Creator.

No one's light outshines another yet in observation some burned brighter.

> **"We are beautiful, healthy, intelligent, creative, giving, loving, intentional … blissful." -Kate**

We come to earth manifested in the physical and our emotions are dominant, not our thoughts. We begin as babies. Even babies tell you what they are feeling … happy, sad, wet, hungry, tired, bored. These are all feelings. When I was in the beginning place, the place of origin, I wasn't thinking … I was feeling.

I felt … loved, complete, whole, right, beautiful, all knowing, abundant … and those around me felt the same. As their energy passed through me and surrounded me it was as if we were all dancing light. Involved in a beautifully choreographed dance of light, without limits and when we crossed into each other we became brighter, more intense and felt each other's divinity and presence. We understood what the other was feeling and it reflected exactly the same to each other. When

we separated our lights we still felt whole … nothing
lacking. It was blissful, joyful, completing one another
with the absence of nothing.

**Abundant, glorious love and fulfillment.
True eternal bliss.**

I was part of all divine lights. I was aware that the
Creator felt joyful bliss while watching us interact in
this playful exchange. I felt His light and love within
me at every moment. I was not separate of HIS light and
love, yet I knew I was somehow smaller. I did not think.
I only knew. I simply *was*. There were no questions.
I was complete, whole, lacking nothing, having all
things. I felt infinite, weightless, there was no place
I couldn't go or be. I was unaware of earth, physical
limitations or time. There were no limits to anything …
knowledge, light, space … nothing. It was all there.
There were no physical aspects to where I was at all.
I've never felt such joy. It was complete fulfillment …
total ecstasy. I was expanding and contracting with my
feelings. I was weightless energy that flowed. I could
see or do or go anywhere by directing a feeling. I was
a bubble blowing in the wind exploring and soaking in
and becoming everything I saw and all I saw was light
against darkness … lightening bugs.

I was fascinated with lightening bugs as a child. How
in the world did they "glow?" I only knew that when

you turned on a lamp that was plugged in it worked but when it wasn't plugged in it didn't.

I just couldn't imagine how these little creatures glowed without a plug. But I remember watching them and chasing them and being so happy as a young child. They must have reminded me of the Creation realm. It made me deeply happy.

> *"You are not separate from anything or anyone. We are all created equally from the Creator. He in us and us in Him."-Kate*

I only experienced this place a little while or maybe for centuries or millenniums.

Then I was "called" to Him, the Divine Force, the Creator. He expressed to me that I was to "become."

In a flash, I was instantly shown what I now know was my entire life here on earth in this realm. It was as instantaneous as a heartbeat. I understood from the Creator my purpose and as a drop of water into a pool sends rings out in to the rest of the water, I was shown the infinite impact of my presence here on earth for generations. All in a second or even shorter, I wasn't afraid, I didn't hesitate or question. I didn't think at all. There was no decision to make. The Creator had shown me what I was to "be" and I accepted it into myself and knew somehow that this was my purpose, my destiny, to become this thing that I now am.

There was only a feeling of knowing. There had been no lack of knowing before this moment, but now that there was a knowing, it was a feeling of yes … only a complete understanding of what was meant to be.

Then I was separated from Him and was hovering in a corner of a room with a grey tint. There was a bright light over what I now recognize as a hospital bed. There was a woman giving birth but I never saw her face. I was in a corner "hovering" over the events below. There were Doctors and nurses around this woman and I realized what I was observing was a baby's birth. Then all of a sudden I could "feel" wet, cold, and the hands of others touching me. I could hear voices and my eyes squinted under the bright light. I *was* the baby. I was no longer in the corner. I was being held by the woman and I had a body. I was physical. It was super weird as I was only intelligence before and now I had a body and could touch, feel, see, and smell. I was a human. It all happened so quickly, and then time slowed down for me. I was so present at that moment. I remember being born. This was in fact my birth, and my inner dialog whispered ever so softly to my heart in this new reality… "I'm here. This is it."

CHAPTER 6

DEJA VU

I've always had such a strong sense of déjà vu—not just a feeling that I've lived exact moments of time, but a deep resonating—yes—breathtaking expressions of what I was shown perhaps. A great knowing that wherever I am is exactly where I'm supposed to be. No matter the circumstances. Neither good nor bad … just where I am meant to be. I remember having a conversation with my late husband and telling him that if he didn't take better care of himself physically that he was never going to make it to 55. He died at age 54. I'm not sure why I chose that exact age when I spoke with him. He and I were in our 40's at the time. It was a premonition that stuck as if I had a strange "knowing." Right before I discovered that I was pregnant with our youngest son, I heard a whisper in my soul that I was going to have another son. It happened in front of the mirror while I was putting on my makeup for the day. I thought to myself how strange that was. I had no knowledge of being pregnant at the time and we weren't trying for another baby. I shrugged it off as just another thought until the ultrasound several months later revealed to us that I was indeed pregnant with a baby boy.

What I came to terms with after my husband's passing was that he had fulfilled his purpose. All of us have a specific purpose to fulfill before we leave this place and Rick had done what the Creator set out for him to do. His *intention* had been fulfilled and he no longer needed to be here with us. Though I continue to wish he were here in his physical expression every day since the day he passed on.

CHAPTER 7

INTENTIONALLY YOU

A potter doesn't make a cup to drink from and then ask the cup what it's supposed to be. He decides what he is going to form from the clay and with that *intention* in mind, he forms a shape of a cup. In the same way, the Creator puts forth an intention and then allows His creation to fulfill that intention.

You can do many things with a cup if asked, the cup might become quite another thing. It may hold pens on a desk, or might be filled with candy kisses for a Christmas gift. Every now and then it's used as a cup for quenching thirst, but then it's washed out and someone puts it in the thrift store pile to give away. It sits on a shelf waiting for another to see its purpose. Someone picks it up one day and decides to put a small plant in it and give it to a friend that needs cheering up. The plant lives for a little while and then outgrows the cup and is replanted. The friend washes the cup out and decides to put soap in it by her kitchen sink. Her grandchild comes in and knocks it off into the sink when he washes his hands and it breaks into small pieces. The woman loved the cup so she glues it back together and decides to use the cup as décor on a shelf. It sits there for many years until the woman passes on. Her family has a garage sale for her things and yet no one buys the cup. The remains of the sale are sent to a thrift store, where an artist picks up the cup and takes it home. She breaks it into pieces and uses it for a mosaic on the top of a table giving yet more years of enjoyment.

You can do, see, and become many things in this lifetime, but you are still YOU. You are not limited when you become a human being thrust from the creation realm. You are given the opportunity to share your divinity with the physical world we call earth.

> *"You were created to be divine and perfect lacking nothing. That divinity does not perish when you are animated into the flesh. Your divine light is only temporarily masked by the physical expression of yourself if you allow it to be."-Kate*

You can feel thrown out and feel unloved by the circumstances in your life, but you still have a purpose. A divine purpose. The Creator allowed this cup to become what it was to be without expectation or complaint. The cup was beautiful just as a cup but was used for many different purposes. Still beautiful and useful in each role. Still a cup which was its intended purpose but skillfully and creatively used for so many different things.

We are all created as human beings. We will always be humans while we are in this physical world, but we are allowed by our divine Creator to become, go, do, explore, see, and be used for many different purposes.

The difference between us and the cup is that we can choose what to be, go, do, explore, see ... become. The recollection of seeing my life in advance ... this brings up a very controversial subject ... pre-destination. Many people believe that our lives are pre-destined, or pre-determined by our Creator with little to no choice in our existence here. The irony here is that both views are completely valid.

You see, the Creator is all- knowing, lacking nothing ... Possessing all future knowledge. In our human forms, we do not understand this concept but when I was with the others −I knew and understood completely. We were one with Him but separate. We were intelligent with all knowledge without thinking ... we were all knowing, yet "under" His jurisdiction. I knew He was bigger than me. We are a part of Him. We have GOD/Creator within us! A reflection but not equal. So yes, our intention is to be humans. Our souls were created to manifest a physical expression, but our choices are made by us in this world. The Creator showed me my life. Was it pre-destined or his all- knowing vision of what was to come? I wish I had all of the answers, but we are learning together on this journey how to reconnect to our origin and that is a question whose answer remains theoretical at this point.

CHAPTER 8

THE POWER OF HUMANS

I inherently "knew" or felt that I was in Him, and He was in me. We were the same but not equal. His light was bigger. It welcomed me and enveloped me and I could flow in and out of this light but it was larger, burned more intensely brighter and I yearned for it. Returned to it and basked in it. The Creator was the sun and I was a grain of sand on a beach. A smaller portion. Still infinite but somehow only a part of this bigger being. I felt safe. Whole. Complete. There were no thoughts ... only conscious feelings. I was able to be a part from myself only to record the experiences I was having in my consciousness. There were no questions. It was a "knowing." It pleases the Creator to see myself and the others interacting, enjoying the discovery of each other ... being there was beauty and intensity to all of us and we were a reflection of one another. Pure love. Nothing negative. It is the same now. The Creator looks upon us and is pleased at how we interact, grow, learn, and discover each other.

In the creation realm there are no negativities … no judgements.

Every being is innately an extension of the Creator and part of you also. There is not him/her or it … only us. It is a dance of conscious existence uninterrupted by self and yet full of self. We are all one.

It is like a drop of water into a pool … the rings infinitely wash outward within it. The drop itself is separate but when it enters the pool it again becomes unrecognizably a part of the whole body of water … joined … within … absorbed. This is how you are before you were you. A beautiful creation—A separate being from the Creator but on purpose. Defined. Full of divine light. You are perfection, loveliness, a reflection of the Creator and He is happy, joyful, proud and enamored with you. There is no fault, nothing you could do can harm your well –being or value.

The Creator doesn't control you … you are totally free.

Do you like what you see?

We are not these ever changing bags of flesh with needs and wants and desires. We are truly organic free spirits that lack nothing. We are intelligence. We are knowing. We are infinite and beautiful beyond compare.

We are light against the darkness and light so brilliant and clear that as human beings we could not even look upon ourselves. We are as young as the universe. We are as old as eternity. We are love. We are everything and everything is us.

> *"Your possibility is the possibility of you. You are your potential. Anything you can think of or dream you can be, become or have. You lack nothing. There are no limitations. The sky is not the limit … for it is an umbrella that protects our world … a covering … the bubble that keeps us and the rest of the universe safely apart to keep order. The truth is there are no limits."-Kate*

You are …
Beauty and beautiful
Courage and courageous
Infinite and infinity
Potential and potentiality
Grace and graceful
Generous and generosity

Do not compare yourself to those around you and / or operate from a place of lack. There is nothing you can't see, do, or have in this beautiful physical realm.

No one else has "your" portion. There is nothing and no one that can keep you from doing what you set your thoughts and ideas upon. Nothing is stopping you. The power to have what you desire is within you and the universe was created to bow at your feet if you obey the laws of it.

The Creator put you into play simply by thinking of you with a specific intention. There was so much focused energy put into just you. Who your parents were going to be … your DNA structure … your spiritual presence and your physical presence here were all set out with intention … cosmic, divine, creative, loving intention. There are no mistakes.

There are no accidents.

Remember that you are a part of the Creator and he has ordained your very life for creating. You can create a different scenario just by putting your intention into it. Focus on what you want, how it would feel to be living the dream that is in your mind's eye and then make choices toward it. Every day, think on it and the "it" becomes bigger and bigger until it is your reality. You have the power to create whatever future reality you want. It's simple. Easy. Life flows when you relax into this idea.

In my very first yard of my very first house, we planted beautiful purple oleanders. I had always wanted those fragrant blossoms to welcome me into a new summer day. I had seen them in other yards and loved their sweet smell and the way the delicate blossoms danced in the wind. We planted them alternately with beautiful white oleanders not knowing that they would/could/might cross-pollinate ... The next blooming season produced a hybrid lavender blossom rather than the deep rich purple blooms that we were hoping for. Was the intention of the Oleander changed in some way? The Oleander is still an Oleander no matter what color it blooms. The intention was a bush that blooms with a certain flower. Had the Oleander bloomed as a rose or a daisy instead, then its intention would have been altered. You are intentional, no matter how many things change in your life. Circumstances, hair styles, jobs, relationships ... you are intended to be a human in your physical expression, observing, learning, experiencing all the delicious offerings on the menu of life.

Every human being was intended, no matter how short a lifespan, or what sort of disability or disfigurement, no matter what ethnicity or infirmity ... the focused intention that the Creator breathed forth into you becoming a human was lovingly intentionally divinely crafted and cannot be altered or changed by your actions.

> *"You are always a divine child of the Creator and you can never be anything else. Release the need for outside*

> *validation ... **Don't write the story of
> your life BE the story of your life.**"-Kate*

Live in your truth. Live your life with the idea that you are divine and therefore, no one can negate your unique presence here no matter what their agenda. Move forward knowing you are on the right track as long as you feel the intuition of your soul saying "yes." If what you are chasing, dreaming, or doing feels "right" then it is! Listen to the sound of your soul and continue on no matter what anyone else has to say about it. Only then will you find your strength, your light, and your destiny. When our minds are quiet we can listen to the sound of our breath and how effortless it is. Focusing upon this, clearing our minds and allowing ourselves to relax out of the hustled confusion of life and into a place where we are calm, quiet, peaceful even ... we can find our true nature.

When we are fearful, we block out the presence of the Creator within us. We become somehow separate from Him. We view ourselves as being out of control somehow, being victimized by everything around us instead of affecting everything around us.

Have you ever been in a room where you could feel the stress? You could "cut it with a knife?" We have all experienced this from time to time. Instead of becoming fearful or anxious, we should wake up the light within and begin to create the feeling of being blessed, happy, powerful, and fulfilled. Is this easy? Heck no!! We are human. We can be annoyed by negative, complainers who seek out to find like-minded people to commiserate and conspire against the unicorn, cupcake, rainbow-lovers of the world as much as anyone. However … the conditioning of our past to become irritated and judgmental of those who were in such a negative energy state can been altered by changing our thought processes, and it is possible to remain calm, peaceful, and resolute. The Creator is with you. You are never lacking. Changing the way you react to a situation changes the outcome. Can you change the others? Not really, however you can change your reaction and lift the energy in the room. When we think with our heart and not with our intellect, we wake up not only the connection between us and other humans, but each time we do this, our heart thoughts become stronger and our egos smaller.

One of my favorite spiritual teachers of all time, Dr. Wayne Dyer once said;

"If you change the way you look at things, the things you look at change."

We are divine, inspired, and safe. That does not change with our surroundings. We are always grounded in the comfort of knowing that we are in Him and he is in us. We are the sum of everything and have the power to harness all of the universe if we wish. The

Creator made the universe in a scientific order to bow at our feet and be commanded in a beautiful energetic dance to create for us the circumstances we wish to have present in our lives. We can think upon a thing, revel in the emotion that it stirs in us, imagine it is so, before it is so, and it will come to us as a manifested part of our experience here.

We are the sum of our experiences, so if we want different experiences, we have the power to create those for ourselves. Once we realize that we were specifically ordained to harness this power, and it is neither egotistical nor narcissistic to live our lives in the truth of this concept, we can think, do, or have anything we'd like to experience here without exception.

CHAPTER 9

BLESSED

Be happy ... it drives people crazy!!!

This life we've been blessed with is uniquely ours. It is exclusively between us and our Creator. At the moment of our first breath until we draw our last, it is divinely and uniquely given to us to experience from the self. If you think about this. Who else's perspective do we have? We share our experiences with other humans, beautifully intertwined in an existence that we call "our lives." Others who share our life are special, drawn into our experience by the fateful hand of creation; set forth before infinity began. I know this because I have met so many people that I know to the depths of my soul that I danced with in that heavenly creation realm. They are a part of my light here on earth and I have felt their spirit before I even met them here in their physical expression.

But if there is one thing I know to be true, it is that we are here to have our unique and beautiful life experience for *ourselves* … it is why we are here in the first place … to experience this realm. We are completely connected to and with every other person on the planet as well as nature and all that has been created for us to enjoy during this beautiful experience we call life as a human. Because we are connected, every decision we make and each choice that we act upon has a direct effect on humanity, nature and beyond. So it is not a selfish pursuit of our inner being. It is however a careful observation of this physical realm while we exist in it. The choices we make to experience this or that and the emotional choices as well affect the sum of all of us … the collective consciousness. So we are here to experience this life from our soul perspective, however we cannot deny the connectedness to the human race, the earth, and nature as a whole. We are undeniably a part of all of it and therefore cannot really ever be separated from it.

CHAPTER 10

MY CONFESSION

During my late husband's illness, I was desperate and stupid and was in denial of his diminishing health. I only saw my love and those piercing blue eyes. I did the best I could to just get through this cancer and death experience without killing myself in those dark moments because I just couldn't take the reality of his illness anymore. I was convinced that I would never make it through watching him die. Would I have to be there? How could I not? Was I strong enough to hold the hand of someone who shared his very soul and DNA with me all of these years and not fall apart? I was going to have to be strong. He was afraid and sad and after all, he was the one that had to do the dying. But he was equally strong and constant. He did what he had to do to stay alive and didn't complain. He is still to this day the bravest person I know. My part would be over soon, or so I thought. In those last days of my husband's human frailty, I prayed, I cried, I bargained, I even laughed for lack of any other emotion I allowed myself to have. I was devastated. We were losing the battle to this murderous disease, this lung cancer that had descended upon us with no cure, no hope, only a sentence of what was predicted to be his last eight to twelve months on the planet and I was going to have to do this. I was given no choice. He was given no choice. Our family was given no choice. I was so frightened of this death experience … all of it. How it would happen, what it would be like, physically, mentally … and the aftermath of my children's grief. He and I were so scared that we didn't even speak of it with the exception of once. How strange that he had this terminal disease and we never talked about it. We talked about how he was feeling this day or that and how he felt treatments were going and that was pretty much it. But this one time … this brief intermission from our ignorance is bliss choice … I walked into our kitchen on an early fall morning and he was making coffee. I greeted him with a good morning kiss and saw tears streaming down his face. I whispered his name with a weak voice full of concern and he pulled me close in a tight embrace and began weeping holding me as if it were the last time he would ever have the chance. We just held each other silently for what seemed like a lifetime and he cried and I cried. Our tears blending together on our hands as we gently wiped each other's cheeks. In that heartfelt moment in the silence of that room, time stood still in this physical world and I felt like we were together once again in the creation realm. We had no need for words because we imbued our emotions for each other. I felt his sadness and desperation with every heartbeat. I know he could feel my heart breaking with every breath. At that particular unforgettable moment, we experienced the depth of our love and felt what each other held in our hearts, separate but the same right there in that moment. We joined our hearts as one without speaking a word. When we finally, reluctantly, released our embrace, still clinging to each other's hands as if to maintain this moment forever, he whispered to me "I'm scared. I'm so scared." "I don't want to leave you alone." "I don't know what happens. Where do we go? Where will I go? I'm not a very good person. I haven't been a very good person." My heart sank back into my chest. I was literally sick at my stomach to hear what he thought his life had been. My soul had yet to experience that level of compassion in all of my 51 years on the planet. I grabbed his face in my hands and expressed my love for him. I assured him that he was an amazing husband and father. He had such a good heart. I pleaded with him to look at the gifts he'd been given. Our children … his legacy. How could he deny that he was loved and blessed and valued by our Creator when given such blessings? I said "God loves you and I love you. I'll be ok. It's going to be okay. Don't talk like this." He continued to weep and shared that he felt that he was abandoning me. He had promised to love me until the end and now he was leaving me alone to have to weather the storm of grief and to care for the broken hearts of our kids and grandkids. He cried for the grandchildren he would never rock on the porch we had always talked about. He wept and spoke of the tender love he had for our grandson and new little granddaughter. At least our grandson had almost 10 months with him. Our little granddaughter was fresh into the world and he wept because he knew she would never recognize his voice to hear him say "I love you little one." He was deeply grieved for leaving his daughters with holes in their hearts and pictures to explain to their children of a man they cherished and adored. He was so desperately grieved that he wasn't going to be able to help his two sons grow into men. He wanted to be there for me and for us, to help navigate those uncertain times. He was desperate to not have to go through what he felt impending in his soul. He was afraid to leave me alone. He felt he had always protected me and that he was leaving me alone and that I would be lonely. I assured him that I would never be alone. That our children would be there for me and that they would never leave me lonely. He grieved the loss of time and how he felt responsible for taking that away from me and his family. He was so sorry. He kept saying how sorry he was as if somehow he had brought this purposely upon us. It was the most heart breaking, gut wrenching sadness my soul had yet experienced here. It hurt so badly to see this strong man, this man I so loved being this vulnerable and this frightened. I could not imagine what his thoughts were. Where they took him. I needed to be strong. I was always the stronger one. Stoic, sometimes seemingly unfeeling … but in truth, completely emotional, feeling everything. Being better at not showing it. My heart was ripped from my chest that day and the depth of melancholy was almost too much to bear. Little did I know what was coming … the fear, instability, rage, and apathy that I would experience as this horrible unfolding of events took place. This was the conversation where I revealed to my husband of 31 years that I had a pre-birth experience. I was trying to comfort him. I was trying to share with him what it was like and how we were created so he would not be afraid. It was a strange coping mechanism that I wanted him to know that I would be alright without him when all I wanted to do was to convince him to stay as if he had control over his disease at this point. I was trying to fit him with armor for his journey and somehow give him the faith and strength to endure what was to come. He sat entranced in the description of it, tears streaming from his face onto his robe. His eyes became brighter as I spoke of the dancing of souls and the Creator's love for us. He re-lived every moment of ecstasy and marveled at the decision I had made to be assimilated into this physical realm by becoming human. I shared with him the "hovering in the corner of the hospital room over a woman giving birth. How I was limitless and weightless and then all in an instant, I was wet and cold and looking up at a bright light as I felt the touch of gloved hands upon my body and realized I was the baby just born." He pushed back the tears as best he could as his face became more relaxed and his entire demeanor changed. He couldn't believe it. Not the revelation, but that he had known me so intimately for all of these years and that I had never shared this memory with him. He once again began to weep and through his beautiful blue eyes now red and swollen asked if I thought he would go there. Would he have a chance to go there? I only replied that while in the creation realm I had asked the Creator if I would get to come back to this place where I felt so much a part of everything, so connected, so loved, and so complete. The Creator had answered me that I would return to this place very soon. I told my husband that I was sure that was the place which we returned to after we had experienced this physical world we now knew as our reality. We felt some comfort together in that moment. He knew I had a special faith that always moved me forward and I knew he understood that this was where he would be going. A dream within a dream. He would pass to this place as easily as he was born into this one. Effortlessly and painlessly. From one dream into another.

Rick urged me to write about my experience. He remembered I had always told him I wanted to be a writer but had never shared the subject matter. I hadn't been encouraged to write of my experience since the sixth grade. I attended Catholic school and in an English class we were encouraged to write about our summer. I was barely 11. I didn't write about trips to Mexico or traveling the country with my parents in an RV which we actually did quite frequently while growing up. I didn't write of visiting relatives in Minnesota which we also did quite frequently. I wrote of the ecstasy of the creation realm where I had friends that lit my soul and of the Creator who thrust us out of himself into a place only lit with the beauty of a trillion souls. I shared my story on paper for the first time. Sister Nancy was a beautiful person. She reminded me of my cousins in Minnesota. She had red hair and a soft china doll skin and blue eyes. She was a very sweet person. Some of the nuns were not of her constitution, but she was wonderful. She was warm and caring and encouraging. She didn't discipline us like the other nuns. She was my favorite teacher. Kind and gentle, and she loved to teach. It was definitely her gift. When we got our papers back, I had a big A+ at the top with a note saying that my paper was "Fantastic! I want to speak with you in private!" Who me? Oh my goodness! Never in all of my 11 years was I ever told anything that I had ever done was fantastic! I was mischievous and got lots of spankings against my backside with a peach tree switch by my Grandma. She was a rule maker and to keep order, she wasn't afraid to swat us when we went out of line. I dearly loved that woman. She was loving and kind and she kissed me a lot and told me she loved me. In a family of ten you have to fight for any attention if you were ever going to receive it and I was so happy to hear that someone loved me without having to perform a nice gesture or beg for attention. With Grandma, it was just freely given, kisses, peach tree spankings and all. I rarely heard that I was special much less fantastic!

But now, Sister Nancy had freely given me a "Fantastic!" Well I was just elated! This was my life's work! I felt special and someone else finally agreed. She encouraged me to write of this when I got older. She told me it was a gift from God and that I was to share it with the world, this message of purity and beauty, inspiration and peace. I remember going to my mother that day and telling her how excited I was about my paper, my bright red A+ and my "Fantastic!" She was proud and asked me what the paper was about. I told her what I wrote and she asked why I hadn't written of the lovely vacation we had been on and why I felt I had to make up stories to write about rather than the truth. I protested that it was the truth and I wanted to write of it because most of the summer, I had spent in my imagination trying to meditate back to that space. She and I butted heads which we would do many times more in our Mother/child relationship. I had told her about the things I had seen on numerous occasions from a very young age, maybe two or three. I spoke with her plainly about the

Creator and the fireflies in "Heaven." She always sort of just listened to my "stories", reacted to them as such, and went about her business. In this particular encounter, because I had made quite public my recollection of the creation realm, she reacted differently than before. She spoke from a place of fear which I completely understand as a parent myself. She told me that if I continued to share my crazy stories with people that no one was going to like me, much less love, me because they would think I was crazy. She said I just had to stop the nonsense and stop telling these "crazy stories." I told her I remembered coming out of her tummy when I was born. I remember because I was up in the air and saw all of it. My ideas were foreign to her and she could not possibly imagine what I was saying to her was true. It was unfathomable to her at that particular time and space and it simply couldn't be true. She was trying to protect me by telling me to never speak of this again. I was 11 and my Mother was my Mother. I never spoke of it again until I shared it with my sweet dying husband to comfort him in his grief in those last days. It was a moment I will never forget. He and I never spoke of it again. I pray in some way that it helped his transition into the next life. I would have given my own life to have traded places with him that day and on the following days. He was such a tender hearted man. He was so very quiet and understanding of things of this world. He was soft spoken. I was loud.

He was observant. I never remembered names or faces and he took account of every one.

At the moment of my husband's death while in my arms, as he finally released his physical body it became an unbelievable moment of clarity for me. Even in my darkest moment of grief, disbelief and unspeakable pain, an epiphany literally opened itself to me. We are one with our Creator and when we experience death in this physical form, it is nothing but a change of place. Our bodies do not release our spirits. *Our spirits release our bodies* and we are again in the place from which we came without the limitations of time or space. We join others who are in that same element and are free. Those we left behind in this physical realm have been touched by us and like our Creator we (our energy) have become a part of them and our spirits have expanded as well. We shine brighter as we reflect the love we experienced here in this world as humans. My family was devastated by my husband's passing. He was the good in all of us. Mild mannered and smart. Always with a smile and a quick wit. He loved his family. We were his life force.

Rick passed on November 19, 2013 at 7:45 in the evening. All of his children surrounded him in our living room, as well as a chaplain and myself. I had my arms wrapped around him as he leaned back on my chest. I was whispering in his ear how much I loved him and that it was alright to move on. I kept saying "It's ok. You're ok." Over and over again. I'm not sure where

I gathered the strength to say that to him when all I desperately wanted was for him to stay. Then in a quiet moment, he released his body and he was gone from us. In the following minutes, hours, days and weeks, we did what was necessary to move forward one moment at a time into the unknown version of a life without him. Never to experience the warmth of his embrace, the sound of his laughter, the house filled with the aroma of his cooking, the sparkle in his eyes when he expressed his heartfelt love for us, or how he danced the same way for 30 years to every song. His time here was finished.

As if in an effort by humanity, itself, to protect us from the depth of emotion felt at the loss of life here, there are no words to describe the pain felt by all of us, especially my youngest son. My husband passed the day before he turned 16. At a time when the other kids were looking forward to driver's licenses and sweet 16 parties, he was experiencing the trauma, chaos and unspeakable grief of losing his Dad and knowing that he would grow into a young man without him. There was no recourse, no restitution that we could barter to have kept him here with us. We were victims of this horrible fate and left with little choice but to move forward through this tragic event. We were powerless to the passage of time. I'm quite sure that if given the opportunity, Rick would say he regretted that he couldn't hang on long enough to get past his youngest son's birthday. He was so connected to his children. He felt as if he didn't deserve them, these indescribably delicious, beautiful humans he in some way had dreamed into reality. They were his heart, his soul, and his very reason for living. He never felt as if he was enough for them. He led them with a quiet, intelligent, soft-spoken hand.

He was no longer living and breathing amongst us and we were devastatingly lost. Abandoned to this world at the cruel hand of fate to continue forward with no other choice.

So given the privilege of this physical realm, his spirit became life. His thoughts and ideas a part of me and his physical attributes, beauty, intelligence, and sincere tender heart, a part of our children and grandchildren. He is not gone. He very much still "is." He is not only present physically through our children but where he exists now, he can be two places at once. Maybe even more.

CHAPTER 11

A MESSAGE FROM
BEYOND THE GRAVE

I was in California visiting a prospective college for my oldest son just 7 weeks after my husband's passing. We stayed with a dear friend whose roommate was celebrating a birthday, and there were other guests in the house. The doorbell rang and as we were all hurriedly getting ready for the celebration, no one went to the door, so I took it upon myself to answer it. As the door opened wide, there standing before me was this beautiful blonde thirty-something. I found it strange that when I first glanced upon her she almost had an ethereal glow about her. Similar to the sun being at the perfect position behind her shining a bright beautiful luminous halo around her entire body. It was the roommate's best friend who had just flown in from London. She was a tiny little thing and very friendly. After our introductions she went in to greet her friend and they chattered and giggled like a couple of school girls catching up after a long pause. After a bit we all found ourselves gathered in the living area of the house enjoying some wine and bouncing in and out of each other's conversations. I found my inner dialog whispering how strange it felt to be drinking wine and laughing in the company of both friends and strangers so soon after this tragic loss, this sorrowful event that had taken place in my life. But I was in fact laughing and enjoying the company of others. It was refreshing and wildly invigorating after the darkness of the events past had kept me hunkering down into my own place of safety from what I viewed as an unsafe world in my new reality. There was a bit of a break in conversation and the beautiful blonde girl with the ethereal glow sort of spoke out and said "Hey I know this might seem strange, but has someone here just lost someone?" Those in the room that knew me immediately glanced over to me as I sunk down in my chair. Those that knew her were a bit hesitant … as if to say "Oh boy, here we go." I was having such a great time. I was actually starting to forget that I had just lost my best friend, my husband and father of my beautiful children. That I was alone and lonely and scared. That I questioned everything because a piece of me was gone and I didn't trust myself as I once did. I felt a sort of embarrassment for being the focus due to tragedy. I didn't want to be "the widow" in the room. I didn't want to share my personal story with this small group of strangers I had only just met. I didn't want or need their pity. I was proud of traveling across the country with my son on this college trek. I was happy that he and I had the chance to laugh, cry and remember his Dad on our road trip out there together. It brought us closer. It brought us healing. We listened to his favorite songs and spoke about the future and the good that lay ahead of him as he began his journey as an adult. He was the one that had the courage to peel me off the sofa several days after the memorial was over and the last of the mourners had gone back to their lives. He had compassion and love and a wisdom that reached far beyond his seventeen years. He woke me up around 10:00 p.m. or so with a soft voice and simply said "Mama, it's time for you to start sleeping in your bed again." I had not had the courage to sleep in the room I had shared with his Dad because of the painful memories that it held, of the struggles of those last months of his life. My youngest son's bedroom was just down the hallway and I called upon him many times for help with his dad during those darker times. These boys, my boys were my strength during this unimaginably difficult time. At their tender ages of fifteen and seventeen, they were forced into being men beyond their years. They saw the tears, the frailty, the strength, the sadness, the love and the faith. They had many conversations with me about their private fears and deep sorrow in what we were all going through.

But here I was with my oldest son who had put away the oddity of sleeping with his mom to provide her comfort and encouragement to sleep in her own bed because the sofa was hurting her back. His tender spirit looked past the ego and acted straight from the heart. He stayed with me until he made sure I was asleep and comfortable and unafraid for three days until I said I could go to sleep myself. I will never forget the humility in those moments. I owed it to my sweet son to be strong and not cave in this moment of "Who has recently lost someone?" How did she know? Who had shared my private information with her? My friend saw the panic on my face and simply answered her that in fact I had lost my husband only seven weeks prior. The beautiful blonde began to explain that she was a medium or physic of sorts. She was raised Catholic and had an aversion to anything like this gift and had spoken to a priest about it on several occasions who had told her not to fear her gift of speaking with those who had passed, but embrace it as a gift of "prophecy." Because of this assurance from her faith, she only shared her experiences in spirit with those who she felt it necessary. So she continued to tell us that a male voice was reaching out to her. She was having conversation with us as well as the voice and she kept sort of giggling, telling us how funny this guy was and that he said his name was "Rich." My friend corrected her and said Rick. She sort of turned her head a bit and then nodded in agreement. She said he wanted me to believe it was him and to prove it he said he always used to call me the "Love of his heart." She turned again and quickly corrected herself by saying "Ok, Ok, No, I'm sorry the "Queen of his heart." Rick and I met when I was 16 and he was 19. We grew up together and experienced all the struggles of youth together breaking up many times and coming back together. Finally after a three year term, we were engaged and when he proposed, he called me the "Queen of his heart" for the first time. It stuck and he continued to call me that for the next 31 years. During our gut wrenching conversation in the kitchen that early fall morning about his death and dying, he called me the "Queen of his heart" for the very last time.

This medium continued to tell me that he wanted me to know that he knew I was grieving and not to worry about him that he was fine and happy. That he didn't hurt anymore and that what I had told him was true. He told me it was just like I had described. He was always there for me and the kids to watch over us and that he wanted me to grieve for a little longer because he "was worth it." Everyone in the room got a giggle out of that one. My husband was very charismatic and this was something he totally would have said in exactly that way. He then said that after I grieve him for a time he was going to send me someone so that I wouldn't be alone. I laughed and turned to my friends and said "Oh hell no, knowing Rick it will be some fat, bald guy with no job." The room was now roaring with laughter. The beautiful blonde girl interrupted us and said that he had one last thing to say and that was that he always loved me, was sorry for hurting me in his human life and that I would know without a doubt, that the one he would send was "the one" so not to worry. And just like that the conversation was over. My breath was forced out of my being in a moment of "No wait … don't go." Everyone in the room was momentarily silent and amazed. We all began our own conversations as I wiped my tear stained face. The others in the room were chattering about and serving more wine as not to embarrass me by looking my way as I gathered myself. You know … in that sort of "Out of respect, let's look this way and pretend we're having a meaningful conversation while she pulls herself together" kind of way. What had I just experienced? What had just happened and how was it possible? I knew what my experience in the creation realm had been like and had faith that we return to this amazing place without limits, but it was difficult still to wrap my head around my dead husband being able to speak to me through this thin vail of reality from his world into mine. It gave me comfort and strength and joy. That experience urged me to push through so many lonely nights before I met the very one he had sent. And even when we met, I wasn't immediately convinced. But as time went on, so many assurances were revealed that I am now certain that the man I had fallen in love with, is in fact the "one Rick sent to me."

CHAPTER 12

THE LONE WOLF

Wolves are some of the most interesting creatures on the planet. They have a highly organized social structure enabling them to enjoy maximum cooperation when hunting, communicating, and defending their territory.

Wolves develop close familial relationships and strong social bonds. They often demonstrate deep affection for their family and sometimes even sacrifice themselves to protect the family unit.

Once a wolf has found a mate, they usually remain together for life.

The Grant family from as far back as I can recall, has always identified itself as a wolf pack. Our family has many wolf-like traits and being so close, would defend one of our own when being threatened. Intensely loyal, extremely focused and traveling often in a pack.

I was left to witness the deep sorrow on the faces of my daughters and comfort the nightmares of my sons. Their lives were confused and set into turmoil over this great loss, as they tried their best to grow into men. In so many ways, I yearned for the release of this life to a peaceful place that didn't have the challenges of waking up to this continual nightmare, however it was not my journey. This was not my fate. But being so entangled in the journey of another and this great tragedy that had befallen all of us was such a great burden to bear. Why had I been targeted as the receiver of such a cruel folly? What had I done to be the unwilling participant in this type of journey? If I truly had seen my life in an instant from the creation realm. Why in the world would I embrace it enough to willfully participate in this sadness, this grief? I had the knowledge of the ages when I said yes … something I do not possess in this human form. How about that ninety percent of our brain that we don't use?

Not so super human as just human am I … this unbelievable challenge and painful part of my life story took me to a place of near insanity. To wake up for thirty-one years next to that face, those eyes, Ugh … his warmth, the tenderness of his touch and his amazing kisses and then for it to be over in what seemed like an instant took me to a depth of grief, pain, and despair that I had previously not even known existed. My desire was to just go to sleep and never wake up. I cursed the morning light as my soul became aware that my reality was in fact that he was gone from me and I was alone. Every day it was a reminder that this tragic, desperate event had in fact taken place. Tears stained my pillow before I even looked at the clock to validate another day without him. Hopelessness enveloped my soul. It was a nightmare relived over and over every morning of every day … it never ended. Desperation was the only thing I could feel. A deep sense of "screw this. If this is life then I hate my life." I resented those who I saw smiling. How dare the sun shine or the children still be laughing on the playground of the nearby school? Didn't they know? How selfish that they live their lives without pause of what was tragically taking place in ours. What my friends thought were words of comfort for me became patronizing, annoying reminders that they would in fact be snuggling their husbands in their warm beds within their lives that had not changed in this tragic, unbelievably painful way. Their children would wake up and choose whether or not to talk to their Dad, taking for granted that he was going to be there forever. Mine would not. Mine would wake up with nightmares and a depth of grief I wasn't sure they could endure. Mine would be desperate to say the things they left unsaid. To say anything at all. To hear his voice once more. To feel his hugs and laugh at his jokes. To taste his cooking and be the daily beneficiaries of so many displays of his profound love for them. Their pain was intensely felt by me and multiplied by the mother gene that kicks in to protect at any cost her dearest hearts. The worst had happened to one of our own and our "wolf pack" would never be the same again. Our alpha male had been ripped from our pack, hunted by the hands of fate. Torn apart by the malicious disease we call cancer right before our eyes. As if chained to a post, we were helpless to the events unfolding before us. Viciously and instinctively protective of each other, the intensity of this experience could have ruined us. We could have allowed his death to tear us apart at the already raveling seams. This was unknown and unfamiliar territory for all of us. I made a lot of mistakes. The biggest one was not crying enough in front of my children more. I chose stoic over genuine. I thought it would help them to think that I was okay when I wasn't. I didn't want them to worry on top of their own grief. I wasn't being my organic self which was to fall apart, be afraid, be confused and hurt and angry and desperate. I should have been more transparent. Oddly enough, the word "parent" is in that expression of our English language. I'd never navigated these waters before as a parent, as a widow, as a woman and I had just lost my counsel, my friend, so there wasn't anyone to bounce my ideas off of. So I sailed through these shark infested waters alone and am not pleased with the way it turned out, however, I have given myself grace and I believe my children have as well. It was more natural to curl into the fetal position and sob through several boxes of facial tissues and throw plates, tear my clothes, shoot the proverbial finger to God and scream until my throat was dry and hoarse. However, I thought that if I remained calm that they wouldn't panic. I was trying to be a beacon of hope for them that maybe things weren't so bad and that life would continue moving forward. It backfired ... I can't speak for them because I respect them too much, but it has been my consensus that they think I didn't love him as much as they did or that I didn't have the depth of feeling that they do because I seemed to be okay when it wasn't okay. It has been several years of deprogramming and getting in touch with the reality of my feelings, expressing them in sound bites as I think my children can take it and sorting things out in more of a realistic scenario to come to the conclusion that I did the best I could with a tragic event and I've forgiven myself for not being perfect. I've allowed myself some grace for not knowing how to lose a husband, for becoming the lone wolf against my will.

CHAPTER 13

A TRIP TO PARADISE

Today, my family is closer than it has ever been. Losing one of us has given all of us a bittersweet perspective on life, relationships, love. We gather every Tuesday at my house for family dinner. Yes, every Tuesday. My children are no longer children as they are nineteen to thirty-two years old and I have been blessed with six adorable grandchildren at this point, so it is a difficult thing for all of us to gather together because we have careers, families, social obligations, husbands, girlfriends … lives. However, doing this gathering is a lifeline to our strength as a family. We are in touch with each other even if just for those several hours of food, laughter, chaos with the toddlers, differences of opinions, and love, that comes from the heart that connects all of us. We make the effort because we want to. We make it a family intention to gather and connect and in doing so, we honor ourselves, our privilege of being born into the same space and time reality, and the loved one who once walked among us. I always share with friends how my kids are so awesome about coming to family dinner that when someone doesn't show up they will get teased via text by the others and sent numerous photos of the delicious food. It's all in good fun. We understand that sometimes things come up and one or the other can't be there, but we always have it no matter who is in attendance.

Here's the disclaimer that I'm not a superhero. I've just overcome some huge life hurdles and had I not had this pre-life experience, I'm not sure I would have survived them. I admire, respect, and covet those who have not had any spiritual experience like mine and have endured and survived even more difficult situations as part of their life experience.

One year had passed since the beautiful blonde ethereal stranger had heralded that Rick would send me someone after I had appropriately grieved him and that I would know that it was the person he sent. Our family was given a beautiful trip to Maui by some amazingly generous friends of ours. They took us as their guests to Maui and gave us the trip of a lifetime with helicopter tours and zip lining, wonderful meals and whale watching tours, one of which was a private tour where we spread my late husband's ashes with the whales as he had requested before he passed. It was a beautiful statement to the kind of people our friends are. They walk as angels here on earth. We had only known them for six months when our children married each other. One month later, Rick received his terminal diagnosis. We were more than stunned. No one had any idea that he was sick. He'd had a cough that just wouldn't go away. Misdiagnosed earlier in the year as an encapsulated pneumonia and given antibiotics, we just sighed with relief and went about our business. These amazing people not only paid for his medical care, but after he passed, they provided me and my sons with a beautiful home to live in without accepting any of my rent checks. They fed, clothed and cared for us … truly the most deeply caring, loving and generous humans I will ever know … And now they had asked us to join them in Maui. They had taken Rick and I there as a celebrate life trip, when he was still doing well enough to travel. Rick was still talking about the beauty of Maui two days before he passed on. And now, my five children three son in laws and three grandchildren all got to go. Our lives will never be the same because of that beautiful respite from reality that was given to us in such a beautiful place. We are forever grateful for our experience. It changed us in such a way that we could deal with our loss in a different light even if just for those two weeks on that gorgeous island. We were refreshed and renewed. It had been fourteen months since we had lost our love, husband, father of five and "Papaw" to these magnificent beings.

We spread Rick's ashes on the last day and then took a drool worthy photo of our family with beautiful smiles and such deep emotional connections emulating from the page that it's palpable.

CHAPTER 14

SOMETHING'S GOTTA GIVE

When we returned home from that trip, it was if someone turned on a switch inside my head. I looked in the mirror and didn't recognize myself. I weighed 180+ pounds on my mere 5'5" frame, and looked so old and worn. No wonder ... I had spent most of the year after my husband passed grieving my loss and spending nights on the couch watching Netflix until 4:00 in the morning while nursing a bottle of wine and snacking on foods I would not normally even think of eating. I woke up, was too tired and depressed and listless to walk upstairs to my empty bed, so I just stayed there on that couch until the morning light broke and again I realized I was alone and sad, lonely, hopelessly grieved and numb from the distress of the life I was forced to lead without him. I faked my way through another day forcibly smiling at those necessary encounters I had to endure in order to do my work, looking forward to the time I could crawl back into that wine bottle that was always there for me as a much needed silent partner, and once again be swept away by the nonsense that I watched on TV.

I thought I was keeping up appearances and saying the right things, comforting those who had witnessed the sadness of it all, encouraging them that things were good and we were strong and brave. Our family was a fortress against the world and in our sheer numbers we were a formidable presence that others admired and were curious about. My three gorgeous daughters were/are my closest friends. Now adults themselves with husbands and children, they were allies in this war against depression and fear. They took care of me that first year with phone calls, lunch dates, cards filled with words of encouragement, lots of hugs and time with my precious grandchildren. Mostly they listened to my complaints of loneliness and fear of the future. They surrounded me creating a shroud of protection from anyone or anything that might bring me harm. To the outside world, we were faithful and stomached our pain like soldiers for the cause. We laughed and took pictures, we gathered for family dinners and held each other's hands and teared up at any memory that surfaced reminding us that we were one short ... always an empty chair, an empty plate, an empty heart ... all the while aching as if our souls had been ripped from our bodies and the very essence of us was gone. This faking an alternate reality was exhausting. It was too much even for me and I was always such a great actress hiding my true feelings about any situation. I was tiring of the masquerade that had become my life. It was like living my life in someone else's skin. Sometimes ignoring reality was the only way to deal with it and at the strangest moments it would rear its ugly head and overcome me like a plague of insanity … I was defenseless and vulnerable to its power of crushing sadness and grief and I would once again be at square one. Disappointed in myself when each monthly anniversary passed. Why was I still so sad? It's been six months … it's been eight months … it's been a year. Time marched on without regard or regret. I was helpless to its constant reminders that I was alone and scared. And I was angry. I was deeply, soul wrenchingly angry. If this was the Creator's way of treating His beloved child then I was not interested in the Creator and his idea for me and my life. Was He this omnipotent asshole that gave me such a beautiful gift of a thirty-one year marriage only to take it away? How dare him give me this once in a lifetime relationship and then rip it away as if it were never mine. He gave it to me and then arrogantly took him back. The Creator sounded more like a selfish child to me. He has millions of others to choose from. Why me? Why him? It was so unfair. So completely unfair. And my children questioned it. When this reality is thrown at you, there are questions that arise about the goodness of others. We all knew plenty of others who were not good people. Why did they get to live and our husband and father had to die? Rick wasn't a perfect husband or father but he was an amazing human being and we forgave his shortcomings, just as he forgave ours. He was so much of a better person than some that we knew who were given the privilege of not dying.

After the trip to Maui, I was in a different place. I had been taken out of my misery to this heavenly place on earth and allowed that peace to resonate within me. But when I got home, things were very different. I knew I needed to break those bad habits of feeling sorry for myself and I had to push a personal reset. I just knew something had to change. I couldn't be this version of myself any longer. I was misery and misery was me.

I looked in the mirror when I got back from Maui and asked myself … actually screamed at myself in the mirror, fists pounding on the countertop, tears streaming relentlessly as usual things that could only spew forth from a broken, frightened widow's heart. I wasn't kind to myself in the things that I said. I wasn't the person I knew I could be. I wasn't a physical expression of what was emerging from the inside. My thoughts turned to the wrong channel and my inner dialog said things like "Now he's gone and you're alone. You're always going to be alone! He was the only one who will ever love you! No one wants to know the real you." I crumbled into a heap on my bathroom floor when I could no longer look at myself, feeling hopeless to how I was going to change. Eyes swollen from wiping tears, and when I couldn't cry any more, I stood up, looked in the mirror and told myself that Rick was sorry for leaving me. He would never have wanted to see me this way. So sad and so mad at myself. I'd done nothing wrong. After all, I'd put on at least 25 pounds of this weight trying to get him to eat those last few months. He was never hungry because of the pain killers he was on, but if I would eat he would eat, so I ate and ate and ate. As if his eating was going to keep him alive. I continued to scream until my voice ran dry. I had hit rock bottom. The point at which I could no longer stand the version of myself that I had become. I was in so much pain and anguish with no way of changing what had happened to me that I felt hopeless. I never dreamed of what was ahead. I was just trying to make it through one day at a time and couldn't imagine a future at this point. Especially a happy one that included a second chance to have a fulfilling relationship. What man was ever going to be interested in a frumpy, old, exhausted, confused, sad, and angry woman like myself? I knew something had to change. I knew I couldn't be this any longer.

CHAPTER 15

PUSH THE RESET

So I made it through yet another sad day of self-hatred and doubt and woke up the next. I knew I had to change my thoughts. I knew I had to change what was going on inside of me in order for things to change outside of me, but how? That is when I consciously pushed my personal reset and changed paths. Through lots of tears, fear and insecurity, I made a decision that I had reached the end of my patience with the way I looked and the way I felt my life was going. In an instant, as quickly as I dedicated my thought to the outcome, I began a journey of self-healing and transformation. I knew I had a long journey ahead and that it wouldn't be an easy one, but I began to reach inside of myself. Meditate, pray, try to find my way back to the way I once felt. Enlightened, fulfilled, without limitation. A place where I burned brightly with the others. I changed my mind and it began to change my life. I told myself "It's time to stop crying. It's time to start doing. It's time for something different!"

Change comes from the inside, not the outside, however to change my inside, I had to change my outside.

I needed a visual reflection of how I wanted to feel inside again.

Beautiful, fulfilled, purposeful, useful, valued.

My faith in our Creator and my divine purpose was the ONLY thing that kept me waking up in the morning. With little sleep, horrible food, tons of wine and negative thoughts running rampant, my body was stressed out, used up and tired of my bad behavior. It was time for me to push the reset and love myself. It was past time. But it wasn't too late.

Had I not been able to assure myself during this devastating time of fear and grief, that what I remembered of my experience in the creation realm was real and true and I was exactly where I was supposed to be and Rick's life played out exactly how it was supposed to according to the Creator's divine plan, I think it may have crushed me. It may have caused an irreversible devastation which I might never have recovered from. But I desired nothing more than to recover. I wanted the sadness to go away. I wanted the self-loathing to stop. I had to start looking outside of myself all the while looking in as well. It was a delicate balance of pushing out that which I didn't want to make way for what I did want.

The very next day after my shouting match at myself, I went to the gym where I had been a member at for over a year at a friend's suggestion. She said I should join and take care of myself during such a stressful time. It was the first time I'd been inside those doors in over a year since I joined. I walked over to the counter like a fish out of water and showed them my badge of entitlement. Went back to the ladies locker room and proceeded to a row machine. One of my best friends is a trainer but lives two hours south of me. She said if I would benefit from one machine at the gym, it was the rowing machine. It's an all over body workout. So I located the two rowing machines that were at the gym, seated myself uncomfortably at one of them and started messing with the adjustable weight and foot straps.

I felt as if everyone at the gym was looking at me. There I was, sitting on a machine with zero confidence, easily forty pounds overweight not knowing what the hell I was doing. I wanted to melt into the floor. I felt so unattractive and stupid. I felt old and irrelevant. All of these little yoga bodies were everywhere. I was rowing at this point. I grabbed the handles and rowed. I thought what the hell. There were others in the gym that needed to lose more than me, but I only saw those younger, smarter, faster yoga bodies that were so on top of their game. Here I was this used up widow with a horrible body image, no self-esteem and fat rolls that wouldn't let me reach the handles on the row machine comfortably. Shit … this was too much. I got in my head and got overwhelmed. I started to cry right there. Oh my God what was I doing? I'm at the gym crying when I already feel like everyone was watching me, pity all over their faces ... what do I do now? It had only been 15 minutes since I walked into that unholy place and now I was leaving!! Oh my God what a loser. I didn't know what to do but the tears kept streaming so I just grabbed my water bottle and almost tripped when I dismounted that rowing machine and walked sheepishly back to the ladies locker room only to find that I had forgotten which locker I put my stuff in. Oh my God this is NOT happening. I was frozen. I was literally paralyzed with fear about having to go to the counter at the front and ask for someone's help. I had to walk all the way through the workout facility wearing my scarlet letter to ask someone to help me find my locker. I was in elementary school again and had forgotten my locker combination for the fifth time. Nuns with scowls on their faces and all. My car keys were in there. I had to go. I had to do the walk of shame ... there was no other way. I waddled my way to the front counter and asked the girl there for some help. In a serendipitous encounter, she was a trainer there at the gym. She told me it happens all the time and to not worry about it. She also asked how I was doing. In an excruciating attempt to seem fine, I replied to her that I was fine and how was she? She said she was good and that she knew my youngest daughter. They had been roommates for a while in college. I had remembered meeting her before but hadn't recognized her outside of my daughter's alliance. This was just awesome! Now it wasn't a total stranger that I never had to talk to again about how stupid I was for forgetting what locker my stuff was in, but it was someone I'd see again and again because she was a trainer at the gym. She was amazing. I was an idiot. Anyhow, without hesitation and making me feel totally at ease, she found my locker and opened it with a magic key that only the privileged had access to and I was once again able to escape the hell I was in and made my way to my car. I cried for another ten minutes in the parking lot in my locked car and then made my way home vowing never to go back to that God forsaken place full of narcissists who had time, money, and freedom to devote to looking at their reflections and worshipping their bodies. Women who had husbands and young people who hadn't lost their Dads. I carried on with my day filled with disappointment in myself and after dinner, wine bottle in hand, I watched some TV and made my way upstairs and to bed. Day two of trying to not hate myself was a flurry of mixed emotions. I got out of bed, had coffee, listened to some inspirational videos on YouTube and then to my amazement, put on my gym clothes and drove back to the place I vowed never again to visit. The girl that checked me in at the desk was the same one that helped me into my locker ... great, how embarrassing. She told me she was happy to see me back in today and asked if I had taken advantage of the free training session with a trainer that came with my membership. I sheepishly replied that I didn't even know about it and she then offered to be my coach. She added into the conversation how sorry she was about my husband's death and that she just loved my youngest daughter and was so sorry she had to lose her dad. I sort of felt that it was meant to be so I took her up on her offer and made an appointment for the next day. What the hell was I doing? Someone that I had to be accountable to? Shit. I'd really done it now. Oh well, it was only one appointment and then I never had to come back. Tomorrow at 9:00 a.m. I could do it. I made my way back to the locker room, made sure I chose a locker number that I could remember and jumped back on the rowing machine. It was challenging and I was breathing hard. The thoughts of negativity going through my head almost defeated me once again, but I didn't cry and I noticed when I glanced at the clock that I had made it on that rowing machine for ten minutes. I started watching what was showing on the TVs in front of me to distract me from myself and then glanced at the clock again. Twenty minutes! My body was sweating and I needed water. Why had I not brought a water bottle? What an amateur. I felt ridiculous as if all of the eyes in the room were once again on the fat old widow trying to work out. I felt like a joke. I grabbed my towel and headed back to the locker room. Grabbed some water from the fountain and left for my day only this time I wasn't as disappointed in myself and even mustered an enthusiastic goodbye to the girl at the counter who was going to coach me tomorrow. Megan. I will never forget her name, her kindness, or her encouragement, during those first few days and weeks at the gym. Over the course of the next month, Megan and I met several times. She showed me how to use the machines, coached me through feeling dumb and insecure and celebrated the loss of my first ten pounds. Wow! A loss that I was excited about ... who knew? It came off rather easily. I guess when you go from couch to gym, your body responds fairly quickly. I noticed my Maui tan was fading. I'm fairly olive skinned to begin with but that south pacific sun had turned my pasty Colorado girl look into a tropical paradise glow and in comparison to my fellow Coloradoans, people noticed. Being tan always makes my eyes look really crystal blue and we all know that brown fat trumps white fat, so I went to the tanning salon and grabbed a three month membership. Here I was a month into my gym experience and I was tanning! Who was I and where had the sad girl on the couch who drank too much wine go? I didn't miss her and I didn't care. All I knew was that I had pushed a personal reset and was changing, improving and the weight was coming off. I looked in the mirror and didn't hate myself as much. And my hair was growing out. I had always wanted long hair but my late husband didn't prefer it and asked me to keep it short so I did. Especially short in his last days by choice because I could get ready in a moment's notice if his health dictated a fast get away.

My dark brown hair was finally growing out. I felt more feminine and prettier as my face slimmed down due to the weight loss. I continued going to the gym. First three days a week and then adding a day for some extra cardio. Then before I knew it I was going to the gym five days a week and smiling at familiar faces as they greeted me in the work out room. Welcoming the loss of over twenty pounds, I had become my worst enemy…a gym rat.

CHAPTER 16

HELLO ME!

My cloud was lifting. Another ten pounds had shredded off my body and my tan skin accentuated my muscle definition. I had also on a whim joined an online dating service. All of the bad things I'd heard about them didn't deter me from trying. After all, I owned a vintage furniture and home décor shop. Where was I ever going to meet a man? It had been in the back of my mind for some time. I finally thirty+ pounds lighter with self-esteem in hand decided that I looked worthy enough for someone to turn their eyes toward me.

And turn heads I did. I'm not sure what the dating pool looked like in my little city, but I was quite popular with lots of emails of interest coming my way. My self-esteem began to repair itself even more. It took every bit of courage I could muster to accept a date with a rather nice looking man named Ryan. He was older and acted like it too. He was the same age as Rick would have been, however he looked older physically and was more

89

"settled." My late husband was a bad ass. He was a Texas boy who had grown up on land and was very capable of almost anything. He could figure out how to do or build anything with ease. He was highly intelligent as well and always beat everyone at Trivial Pursuit. He possessed a well -rounded personality that attracted those around him. I couldn't settle for some old guy that lacked my late husband's spit and vinegar, so I had a nice time, accepted a second date because I questioned my first impression of him but then gently and politely turned down a third date to pursue other gentlemen. I continued to date almost as if it were my job. I met so many nice guys.

I had also met a new friend at a local martini bar. It was classy place and the bartender was/is the best I'd ever encountered. The guy that never forgot a name or a face. Rick would have liked him. They would have had great conversations as well had they gotten the chance. Anyway, my new friend was a beautiful blonde lady. I was supposed to meet another girl friend that didn't end up making it, but figured I was there already so why not order a drink. She saw me come in the door and observed that I was alone, then walked over to introduce herself. She was definitely one that I had met in the creation realm. She was so friendly and as our friendship has developed, I know we were meant to be close. Soul mates for sure. I shared my life experience with her and she shared hers with me as time went on. I was a widow.

She was getting a divorce. Both single in different stages of life. Our friendship flourished and I continued to date. The Creator had provided me with a new light in my life. A new perspective just when I needed it. Many of my friends although supportive of my new found physique and confidence level, had discouraged me from getting too excited about meeting "the one" online. Some had tried online dating without much success and were sure that I was wasting my time and being naïve about the experience. I had declared earlier in the year when it came time to push my personal reset that I was going to be in a romantic relationship by the end of the year. "I am going to manifest a beautiful romantic relationship. My second chance. It *is* going to happen." Many of my friends laughed and thought it absurd of me to believe I could just *think* a man into my life. They counseled me, as if I wasn't familiar with reality, on the ridiculousness of thinking I could manifest a relationship into my life when they had been single and "at it" for many more years than I, to no avail. Their fear was that I was somehow desperate and was going to throw away the wisdom I had collected over the years in exchange for poor choices based on acceptance. They were well meaning, but didn't share my thoughts on creating the life that is in your heart. Little did they know that I was falling in love … not with someone else, but with, myself. My new friend was the light that supported my vision of this new dream and this future relationship that was in my head. She was kind with a true heart and was/is such a good listener. God had dropped her right into my life at just the right time. She has added so much joy and friendship to my experience here and I am forever grateful for her considering me into her inner circle. I was dating a lot and making my choices of what I liked and what I didn't like. I was observing and learning and experiencing life as never before. I had been with my husband from such a young age and never experienced dating at all really. We were together off and on until we got married. I never really dated anyone else. I was having so much fun. I was experiencing and developing my female personal power like never before. I was buying new clothes to fit my newly acquired figure … mostly dresses. I loved dresses but had not made a habit of wearing them before. I had longer hair and was wearing dresses and heels. I hardly resembled the woman that was screaming at herself in the mirror earlier in the year. This journey was unfolding as I took each step forward toward a different end. My daughter's now lovingly refer to this stage of my life as the "Martinis and miniskirts phase."

I was getting up at 5:00 a.m. and meditating and praying on my deck, coffee in hand. I was making lunch dates and dinner dates and girlfriend dates. I was open to whatever was being brought into my reality as I journeyed through this interesting time and space. It was beautiful and true, imperfect for sure, but it was my time to heal. A time to pull myself inward and protect the new me, the real and true me. I was finally healing. I was becoming happy again, but I was still longing for my broken heart to be filled with love and hope and a new romantic relationship. Had it not been for my experience in the creation realm, I might not have had the patience to know that my life was unfolding exactly as it should. I was in the exact space and time that I was destined to be in. I was on a journey of self- discovery, I was becoming aware of who I was meant to be. I was healing from this devastating incident and not allowing it to define the rest of my life.

> *The 13th century poet, Rumi said,*
> *"The wound is the place where the Light*
> *enters you."*

I was definitely wounded and definitely in need of light!

CHAPTER 17

THE STORY OF US

So I met this guy on an online dating service. It was February 22, 2015. I was up doing my usual work, getting on with my day and got a notification on my phone that my photo was liked and I got a wink. It was from a guy named Roger. His name was reminiscent of a black and white movie. Romantic, classic, and old fashioned. I was intrigued. I had no idea what he would look like when I opened his dating profile. He was good looking. Tall dark and handsome … just my type. His written profile was very interesting, and as he described himself, I could sense a bit of a dry wit. I could tell he didn't take himself too seriously. He seemed to have a great sense of humor, and I missed that part of my life so much … Rick's sense of humor. So I decided I'd like to meet him. We arranged to meet that evening even though it was a blizzard outside! Poor Roger! I didn't know he had just moved from California and didn't have much experience driving in the snow or I wouldn't have made him drive across town to a little pub that is within walking distance of my house ... oops. He was a surfer and was most comfortable on a beach. Completely out of his element in the blizzard snow that was falling outside in the distance between his place and where we would meet. Well, he made it and after four hours of interesting conversation and getting to know each other, we hugged in the parking lot and said goodnight. We decided just to hang out again as friends ... nothing romantic ... just to get to know each other better. I wasn't ready for him and he certainly wasn't ready for me!

For the next several months we texted, chatted on the phone, and met for lunch, the park, cocktails etc. Three months later, at Roger's request, we took it to another level and actually went out on a date! It was a romantic evening filled with wine and conversation, great food and a kiss goodnight that would change our playing field and lives forever! He had lived in Napa for a bit and his best friend was the head winemaker at a very celebrated winery there. He knew a lot about my favorite indulgence! What was there not to like? We once again talked, laughed, flirted, and got to know one another very well. Only this time was different. You need to understand here that Roger was my "guy" friend. Over the past several months of our friendship he had listened to me rattle on at lunch and over text about my latest affair and he was solid. He listened, gave sound advice as every girl needs, and we left it at that.

But he had talked me into going out on an actual date, saying that he wanted to get to know me in a different context. This guy was ballsy, brave, and intelligent. He was an amazing communicator! So I said okay. After our "date" was over, and as we discussed over text, if we were going to take it to the romantic level, he would have to kiss me. Fair and square we made a deal. If he kissed me and it didn't motivate us toward a romantic relationship, then we would act as if it had never happened and leave it at that. If we weren't "feeling it" then no harm done. I didn't want to lose my newfound friendship with him. He was adorable, warm, funny, and friendly, handsome, and communicative. What the heck was I thinking keeping him in the friend zone? How had I missed it? Anyhow, after dinner we walked into the parking lot of the restaurant, and I was so nervous. You know the kind of nervous that happens when you are having a baby. You have committed to this and know you have to go through it but you just think at the last minute how you can't do it and don't want to. Ready to make deals with the devil sort of nervous … That kind of nervous.

So we made small talk by my car and then I had enough liquid courage to just blurt out … "Well are you gonna kiss me or what?" (Insert nervous as a school girl here) … oh my gosh! Did I feel like an idiot at that moment? Remember I'm a Texas girl with a lot of sass … I mean a LOT of sass and I just asked him to do the very thing that I thought would ruin our friendship!

He answered like the Jimmy Stewart gentleman that he is ... "Would you like me to?" and with all of the calm, confidence I could muster, I simply said ... "Yes."

Well, that kiss ... Oh my goodness that kiss. Let me explain. You know the moment you realize you shouldn't have enjoyed those last few sips of alcohol, or when the anesthesia places you somewhere between reality and a dream ... you sort of have this out of body experience, like "Is this really happening to me sort of thing?" It was surreal. Only this time I didn't want to hug the toilet and make promises to God that I was never going to keep. It was heavenly. Warm, intentional, emotional.

Ok ... multiply that by 100 and that was how I felt. He didn't just like lean over and lay one on me. This man, this 6 foot 3 inches of tall handsome man leaned in and placed his hand on the small of my back, drew me in and with the other hand caressed the back of my neck and ever so gently and passionately kissed me like I had never been kissed before. Romantic. Intentional, warm and flirty, lip sucking, movie worthy, you gotta have more of this kissing sort of kiss!

Ok ... let me explain for a second so you can collect yourselves. I had been kissed. I had kissed many frogs, toads, princes even, but I had *never* in my entire life been kissed like this! My knees went weak and suddenly I was sort of out of my body. I really have no explanation whatsoever. I just know that until that moment I felt like I was in control. Suddenly, I was willing to surrender not only myself, but everything that was my life to this kiss. So I did what every 50 something not so sure of herself, but overly confident as well would do … I took him home.

My creative, fun & spontaneous nature mixed well with Roger's analytical, sweet, intellectual side of his Gemini personality to create the most romantic, adventure.

Meeting my family was a big deal, not knowing how this new romance was going to play out, Roger and I were careful in the timing of him meeting my friends and family. For the longest time, Roger had a secret name in my phone … it drove my kids crazy that I wouldn't tell them anything about this new romantic interest as I had been on dates before and spilled those beans. But this was different. Roger was handsome and funny, kind and intelligent, had a diverse life experience and was such a great communicator that I knew I was in trouble … I was falling in love. So meeting the family was a HUGE deal … it was well planned and thought out. Roger and I discussed how it would happen and envisioned the proper way for him to meet the clan … NOT!

My family met Roger totally by accident! A month into our serious dating experience, I was babysitting my grandkids so that my daughters and their husbands could go to an outdoor concert. I love the way my girls hang out together. They are three peas in the pod. They talk with each other every day. They are in each other's lives. They're concerned and connected, lifting each other up, providing a safety net that can only be understood by having a relationship with a sister.

Roger had come by the house just to hang out for a bit and he was sitting at the bar in my kitchen while I washed dishes when the girls walked in with the kids almost an hour early! You should have seen the looks between us ... panic? I didn't know whether to tell him to duck out the back door or act like a delivery guy! But in true Roger fashion ... he remained calm and simply said "Well this should be interesting!"

So I introduced my family to my "friend" Roger and then he proceeded to start playing with the grandkids on the floor ... Heart emoji's for days were coming out of the girls' eyes! Still, I stood strong and didn't admit until the appropriate time that Roger was more than just a friend. Apparently Roger and I were the topic of conversation to and from the concert that night. One of my daughters admitted that they were wondering why I wasn't dating a nice guy like Roger!

That summer was a blur ... literally for Roger as he had some eye surgery that left him with the pirate patch over one eye for quite some time. I did a lot of the driving while Roger healed and then got sick myself with my yearly summer cold ... Roger nursed me back to health in the sweetest way ... making home -made chicken soup, covering me with blankets on the sofa in front of his TV and providing his own home cure …

You guessed it! Whiskey and animal cookies. You know … the kind with the pink and white icing with the little sprinkles on top. Normally I don't do a lot of sugar, however I was feeling so sick and vulnerable so I said I'd try anything to feel better … what do you know? An hour later Roger and I were chatting it up and watching one of his favorite movies of all time … "Despicable Me."

After we were both on the mend, there were lovely trips to San Luis Obispo and Napa. The ocean view from our suite and the sound of the waves made for quite the romantic backdrop. Roger surprised me with a bucket list item in Napa one morning by taking us on a hot air balloon ride over the vineyards. It was the surprise of a lifetime and one that we both will never forget. Experiencing that for the first time together has been a sweet highlight of our relationship.

Neither of us prefer heights and the balloons can be unpredictable as they soar with the wind currents. The pilot even warned us that they never know where the balloon will land! Still, we managed to climb on board for the experience. We held tight to each other … clenching really, then took to the skies.

So one of the great things about being "of a certain age bracket" when you meet your significant other is that you don't have the whole … "Could he just learn to pick up his socks" or "I wish she didn't mind me taking time for myself" stage. We were both well- seasoned life travelers when we met and so we had very little to adjust to in terms of compatibility when we were one on one. Roger had to do some adjusting to my big fat happy family life and the demands of my career, and I had to adjust to dating a Gemini which is both enchanting and unpredictable at the same time, as well as some of the habits that come with a bachelor's life. But for the most part, our relationship was seamless ... loving, nurturing, caring, humorous, quirky, spontaneous and deep. Once we committed to each other exclusively and began our journey of discovery together, we were a team ... Just us against the world ... One of the strongest points of our relationship is our relationship "rules." I would call them more "agreements."

- Be relentlessly honest and always trust ...
- Always be kind to one another and act in service of one another
- Never criticize with words or see your partner with a critical eye
- Always use love and respect when talking to or talking about one another
- No matter what ... have each other's backs
- We're on the same team

We found that laying out the ground rules of where we were and where we would be going together in life set a firm foundation of love, trust, friendship, respect and loyalty. Those are the often unspoken agreements of our relationship that have made it so strong, so unique and so blessed.

So Roger and I met on February 22, 2015 ... 2-22-2015. Since that first meeting on 2/22 ... the number 222 has occurred many times. The first trip we took together landed us in a resort room with the number ... you guessed it ... 222. Seats on airplanes have been in row 22 and we have had tickets from everything for the movies to food pick up with the numbers 22 or 222 on them. This number continues to show itself in our everyday lives.

The numerology number 222 is a family, harmony, and relationships number.

The 222 essence includes health, healing, and domestic activity. Love, beauty, and comfort are important, as are relationships, romance, teamwork, companionship, and diplomatic efforts for maintaining harmony. But the family is most important of all.

222's energy is a caregiver. Its maternal nature extends beyond the immediate and extended family to society. There is an urge for everything to be ideal, an ideal 222 sees as benefiting society and humankind as a whole.

The number interacts well with others; it thrives in relationships of any type so long as the relationships are harmonious or can be made that way.

The essence of the numerology number 222 includes romance, healing, comfort, maternal nature, guidance — ideas related to a happy home, family and neighborhood. There is responsibility, love, self-sacrifice, protection of family members, sympathy, and compassion.

On a fun note, in numerology Roger's Life path number is eleven and mine is twenty-two.

CHAPTER 18

LOOKING FOR SIGNS

The number 222 was one of many signs in our relationship to this day that have guided, and comforted me to the conclusion that Roger is the one in fact that Rick sent. It's an oddity, not a coincidence that a week before he and I met, Roger had been contacted by a beautiful lady on the same dating site we met on who had asked him if he would consider an "older" woman. On this particular site you can set your age parameters and his pre-determined parameters did not include this woman's age. So at her request, he did extend his age parameters temporarily to include this lady's profile so that they could interact. Although he went on a date with this lady, it never led to a second date. In the meantime, since I was also of this lady's age bracket, my profile popped up on his daily matches. And there you have it!

There are no accidents. This was a sign.

I continued on this road of self- discovery, dating Roger exclusively, with my secret in hand but never spoke of it with anyone since I shared it with Rick in the kitchen that one fall morning. I knew where I came from and knew that somehow I could connect to that place. I wasn't a medium or a channel or had any special "gifts" in that regard, however I just knew that I could somehow connect with where I used to be. The one I truly am. I wanted to be free again. I wanted to be that lightning bug that flowed in and out of the others. I yearned to be at peace. I meditate, and with focused intention, take myself to that beautiful, blissful place of total freedom. I reconnect myself with the Creator and settle into the feeling of floating freely in this space. I do my best to make time for these moments every day.

I didn't share this secret with Roger for some time. I was falling in love with him, however, I trusted the message from the beautiful, blonde, ethereal girl I met in California who told me that Rick had said specifically that I would know without a doubt that the one he sent for me was "the one." I was given lots of signs along the way, however, I wanted to be careful. I had a family who had met this guy. They knew we were dating. They knew I had dated a dozen or more guys that they had never met, so this one must be special. He played with my grandchildren and we were always together. I felt safe, loved, excited for the first time in a very long time. But I had all of these beautiful beings that relied on me to make a good decision. They had experienced enough grief, trauma, heartbreak with the loss of their Dad. This was a HUGE decision weighing heavily upon me and I couldn't screw it up. I didn't want to date someone and then if something went wrong ... break up. Another loss for them and their children? No. I wasn't willing to risk it. I was keeping it very casual on the outside, all the while falling deeper and deeper into this man. My sweet little grandchildren wanted to sit in his lap. The sound of his name flowing from their little mouths was like the first taste of a snickerdoodle just out of the oven ... sweet, warm, indulgent ... I couldn't get enough of it. I hated all of the insecurity ... the questioning ... Was this really "the guy?" Was Roger really the one that Rick had sent? I needed proof. I was vulnerable and frightened of my own decision making skills. Was I capable of making a true decision on my own without the counsel of my husband? Could I really make such a life changing decision on my own?

THE CORAL SHIRT

So family dinner at the Grant house is a big deal. It's almost always home cooked food. We start with hors d'oeuvres and end with dessert, so it's lots of conversation, laughter, libations and food! Roger was invited to his first family dinner. I cannot imagine what was going through his head. Never being married or having children of his own, he was walking into the lion's den ... the wolves' den actually. He had met the kids before as "my friend."

However now we were deeply, romantically involved and the energy had shifted from "What a nice guy" to "What do you want with our Mom?" (Insert uncomfortable laugh here.) There were going to be some challenges. Remember that Rick had spoken through the lovely "medium" that I would know without a doubt, if the man I was dating was the one he sent for me. Nothing could have spoken more clearly than that first family dinner. Rick had a great coral colored shirt. He loved that color. It wasn't peach, it was deeper, and richer … the perfect color to reflect those gorgeous blue eyes of his. Before we left for Maui to spread my late husband's ashes, a friend of mine who was also a widow, had helped me fill nine individual bottles, full of said ashes, as required by the airline when traveling with human remains. Ugh! I could have lived my entire life without knowing how to travel with human remains. Anyhow, I had wrapped a love note from "Dad" around each one with a piece of his favorite coral shirt. It was a Columbia brand and he always wore it with his khaki cargo shorts. All of us remember him that way and how handsome he considered himself in that silly shirt. He absolutely loved that damn shirt. I had trouble cutting it up but felt it was that one instantly recognizable reminder of this man we loved so much. It brought back so many great memories. Where he'd worn it, how many times he was looking for it when it was in the wash, the baby spit up from our first grandson. All of the sweet reminders of how fortunate we were to be grandparents together before he passed.

So back to family dinner. I am sure that Roger was super nervous, although he never showed it. His calm nature is one of the things I love most of all about him. He is an earth spirit, grounded and solid. I am an air and fire spirit, always changing, jumping around from project to project, and quick to react. So we are all out on the deck chatting and having a great time and in walks the "friendly stranger" that was my guest at family dinner. The kids all recognized the significance of this event. This was the one I had chosen from all the other candidates. He was "the one" or he would never have earned the right of passage into our intimate family gatherings. They knew he was coming. They were expecting it and I had asked them to be on their best behavior and not to devour him but to welcome him into our wolf pack. This is the one. This is the guy. We had known each other six months and dated for three and it was time.

As if the universe picked up an all-knowing paintbrush and placed upon the canvas of life the one instantly recognizable piece that could calm our uncertainty, and imprint him into the hearts of my family … in walks Roger to his first family dinner.

Khaki shorts, coral Columbia shirt and all.

In the words of my late husband, "You could have heard a fish fart" in that moment. My daughters didn't know whether to laugh or cry. Was this some sort of cruel joke? Here was this man who was dark headed like their Dad with facial hair like their Dad and blue eyes like their Dad wearing the same shirt as their Dad. Not only a shirt that their Dad had, but his *favorite* shirt.

Was this man so manipulating that he researched pictures of my late husband on the internet and then dressed like him to evoke a feeling of familiarity? What the hell was going on? Those thoughts would have a place for sure in the minds of others. But not in the minds of my family. You see, they had heard the story that I could hardly tell without uncontrollable tears of the man their Dad would send. And they knew at that very moment that it indeed was Roger. His choice of attire was made glibly at best. He had owned that shirt for years and often wore those khaki shorts. Was the reason he had chosen to wear it that night a coincidence? Not at all. It was a thought whispered into his ear by my late husband that knew my family would respond exactly as they did. They treated this moment as one of assurance and grace. Their Dad used the clothing of this new guy to assure them that the man who appeared in that handsome coral shirt was indeed the man he had sent to their Mom so she wouldn't be lonely, and to stand in as the new grandfather to children he himself would only know from spirit.

CHAPTER 19

THE CATERPILLER

So I have always been fascinated with the quote

"And just when the caterpillar thought her life was over, she became a butterfly."

It was written or said by an anonymous person with lots of wisdom I'm sure. It's one of the truest observations that has ever been made. Think about it … a caterpillar is just hanging out on a leaf eating and eating and eating which is the only job of a caterpillar, (Oh how I want to come back as a caterpillar!) and then all of a sudden it starts to shed its skin over and over, losing its appetite and then is suddenly prompted to hang upside down and spin a cocoon. The caterpillar would think its life was over because life as she knew it truly was. No more scooting on the green leaves of life, devouring, savoring and eating in a blissful state of being. Now her life was totally and literally spinning out of control. It was getting dark. Everything was out of perspective. Nothing was the same.

What a pertinent quote to parallel my very own life story. In the cocoon, the caterpillar found it dark and cold. She was lonely and felt vulnerable. It was unfamiliar to her as she had just been minding her own business and eating her way through life as was her mission. One day, not of her own desire, there was a sudden change, and now she found herself in this dark space, frightened, alone, cold and unsure of her future. She thought she was dying. The darkness encapsulated her spirit and she was disconcerted, lost even. Then things started to happen and she was no longer content to stay the same caterpillar that she was before. She knew something had to change and was changing. She didn't understand what was happening to her, but had no control over it. She stayed in this unfamiliar place and with all of the faith that was left in her, continued on because her life in fact was not over. It had very drastically changed for sure, but she was still alive, even if greatly changed. So she "hung in there", pun intended, and did not die. She allowed herself to be numb with the grief of losing the life she once had, and somehow hope that her life was not yet over. She allowed the changes that were being forced upon her to just happen. She surrendered. And then one day, as if waking up from a dream, a light began to show itself, just a bit. There was indeed a light! Then more and more of it began to seep into this darkness and like a miracle of transformation, when the cocoon broke open, she could see, so much more clearly than before. Her body was changed. Strange and uncomfortable, she opened these things that yearned to be unfolded and once acclimated, they stretched open with the freedom to take her places she had never even allowed herself to dream about. She looked at the world, in a different, new and exciting way. She glanced down upon the trees she once was crawling upon for sustenance, and they looked so small and so confining. She no longer had to crawl. She had earned the freedom through her suffering to soar above the ordinary life of a caterpillar and be lifted by the breezes to another level of existence where she tasted the sweetness of life. Felt the presence of the other beautiful winged creatures like herself and joined with another to create a likeness of herself to continue on after her journey here was completed.

When I broke out of my own cocoon, the light came in through the wounds that I had suffered and after a while, when my eyes could adjust to the new light, there was Roger standing in front of me. He offered me strength to expand my new wings. Support so that I knew I could fly and a deep resonating love to encourage my newly developed inner and outer beauty.

Roger has been a delicious slice of my life experience here. A delightful second serving of love, trust, and fulfillment. Because he was able to put his ego aside and truly see me in all of my human imperfection with all the struggles that accompany five children, three sons in law and six grandchildren who are only his newfound family by default, he was able to embrace us in our uncertainty, and connect with us at the soul level. My life has been forever changed, actually blessed in ways that could only have been ordained by the hand of eternity. A surprisingly pleasant second act to a tragic intermission in the story of my life.

"And just when the caterpillar thought her life was over ... she became a butterfly."

I had no idea how much that saying would resonate within my life and being. I really thought my life was over. I went into this darkness that was so unfamiliar and uncomfortable. My family and some close friends helped form a cocoon of protection around me so that I could endure the changes that laid ahead of me. While my experience on the inside was one of fear, doubt, and uncertainty, I needed that cocoon. I wanted that protection from a world that was once filled with joy, hope, and comfort, but had now become a place of vulnerability, fear, and distrust. Once I was healed and was ready to break free of the constraints of the unknown, I emerged a completely different self, one that was more alive, more beautiful and more grateful for not dying than the self I was before.

Just like the larvae stage of a butterfly, I wasn't thoroughly developed. I wasn't ready to be this particular version of myself. I had to endure death, loss, grief, change, loneliness, anger, and despair. Followed by hope, faith, and the confidence that comes only with surviving the worst. Only then was I ready to break free of the wounds of the past and re-emerge a different, more "upgraded" version of myself. I did in fact think my life was over ... and then, by grace, I in fact, became a butterfly.

CHAPTER 20

PENNIES FROM HEAVEN

Rick is gone from us in physical form, but he is alright. He abides in a place I know very well and in a space of complete understanding. He wishes for my happiness and has the ability to come in and out of my human physical experience here as much as he desires. He is happy and free and rejoices in my emotional well -being. He wishes I still had the eternal knowledge I once possessed from where he abides because I would not question or falter. He wishes my life was easier and that I shared his perspective. He drops pennies from heaven. He leaves me pennies everywhere. He used to pick up pennies wherever we'd go. He read once about a millionaire who always picked up pennies. The friend of the millionaire asked him why a man of his financial status would care about a penny on the ground. The millionaire shared that pennies remind him that no matter how small we feel, we still count and that small things add up to large things.

I can hear Rick's voice as clear as day saying "Find a penny pick it up and all day long you'll have good luck." A silly superstition but one that he has carried over into the next world to remind me that he is still present though not in our physical realm. He does still live! He used to keep a jar of change in our closet. He would unload his change into a big glass jar and celebrate the day it was full. One time he cashed his change in and took our family to Disneyland. Small things do add up to big things.

Since he passed from this life, Rick has been with me on so many occasions. He has left me so many pennies. A penny will just appear in a magical way out of literally nowhere. Even as I experienced the challenges of writing this book, I found pennies to encourage me to continue forward with it. Whenever I am in doubt, having trouble with a situation in our family, or wondering if I can make it through another day without him, he leaves me pennies. He tells me I am on the right path. He assures me I have what it takes to finish raising my teenage boys into men. He whispers to me that there is comfort from a place we are not, however the power of that place is with us all the time. The pennies are a physical reminder that we are never alone. He is in some form of the place that we all originated from. He is in that very place where everything is peace.

CHAPTER 21

CREATION REALM REVISITED

The bible says in Jeremiah 1:5 "I knew you before I formed you in the womb; I set you apart for me before you were born; I appointed you to be a prophet to the nations."

Imagine the beauty of a starlit sky that surrounds you infinitely in every direction. You are floating in its entity. You are a part of its energy. Your first awareness is observation of your surroundings and the feeling of being thrust out into this blackness illuminated only by the lights scattered across it like a trillion stars. You are weightless and fluid moving with every thought effortlessly through this new space. You are form but without body. You are molten lava floating freely. You are aware that there is light radiating from inside you, a warm energy that emanates from within. Your awareness takes you outward and you turn to envelope yourself in the brightest white light shining from an enormous sphere of energy, flowing in and out of itself. The energy from this "being" is fixed upon you. Its' energy is so brilliant that there is an inexplicable gravitational pull toward it and you are suddenly aware of emotions for the first time. This brilliant "being" is the same only the perspective is of a grain of sand compared to the sun. It is huge and overpowering and you become effortlessly overwhelmed by the love, adulation, joy, and utter delight that this being has for you. Somehow, you know this is your Creator and He is pleased with you. Once you experience this acknowledgement, like a blissful child, you drift happily in this new space completely fascinated with just being "alive," not trying to figure out who or what you are. There is an innate knowledge of this space and your place in it.

You gaze upon the light shining from the others and as you fix your gaze on one, a burst of light shines forth like the twinkle of an eye and draws you in. As you thrust toward it in a gravitational pull of curiosity, the light shines brighter and warms your being. You can feel emotions welling up inside you... pure ineffable bliss. It envelopes you and as you approach the light, you are gently swirled into it and become a part of its energy. As if embraced by its entire being. You then see a human face, recognizable yet never having seen it before, angelically smiling at you, completely enamored, simply delighted and in utter ecstasy because you are in union with them. At this moment, you realize you are one of these brilliantly shining entities.

With childlike abandonment, you swirl and envelope each other, reveling in this beauty and bliss and you feel your inner being growing larger and more beautiful, brighter and more aware. When inside this union of souls, completely captivated by the experience, time, although it doesn't exist in this realm "stands still." There is so much focused energy that nothing else exists outside of it. While joining the other "soul", you are sharing your essence with them and them with you, and you leave this union brighter, more beautiful and increased in your awareness. You have experienced the radiance of each other and have shared each other's spirits. You give of yourself, yet grow larger, taking away a beautiful piece of their essence and leaving a portion of yourself with them.

This experience repeats itself over and over in a blissful dance of emotional fulfillment, bliss, love, and peace. You are then called to the Creator. There are no words, only the thought that you are to stand before Him and instantly you are there. In this communion, you understand it is time for you to "be" something else. It is revealed to you in an instant what and who you are to be. As if the space you are in is actually a sort of clear bubble that when stretched open, you view your entire life on earth within it. You acknowledge this new beginning and know that this is who you are, and feel oddly that you've always known it. There is a moment of sadness when you realize that you will be away from this beautiful place with the others, so with only a silent conversation with the Creator, you ask if you will ever return to this place and He simply answers, "Soon." With a resonating "yes," you are hovering in a dimly lit room observing a woman on a table with people around her wearing gloves and masks, and long white jackets, or dressed in white uniforms. You understand the woman is giving birth. When the baby comes out of the womb, you immediately feel cold and wet and the light above hurts your eyes. There are hands touching you and sounds are unfamiliar. You begin to gasp for air and a loud noise comes out of your throat. Realizing you are the baby, there is a deep resonating sense of peace, knowing that you are exactly where you are supposed to be...

We have all come from this place. I'm sure of it. When we close our eyes and breathe deeply focusing only on the gratitude, love and light within us, we reconnect to our Creator, the source of all reality within this human earthly plane. When meditating upon this divine origin, we remember to love ourselves and radiate that love, without hesitation or ego to others who share our time here. Allowing ourselves to reconnect to the blissful, beautiful, energy from which we came, places our hearts in a space of peace so that the true essence of

others is easily revealed. It is through that connection
with source that we are fully empowered to embody
our true intention, reveal our organic selves and carry
the light that burns brightly within us to others in this
place. We are once again free to delight in the wonders
of this world and co-create an experience here that serves
our higher purpose.

I don't remember anything after this until I was
about two years old and my mother was nursing my
little baby brother and I was playing on the floor in front
of them. They were in the rocking chair. I remember
falling down and wanting her to pick me up and comfort
me. I was crying yet in an adult inner dialog, wondered
why she didn't understand that I needed comfort and
why she just continued to nurse my brother. I remember
my inner dialog saying "Woman comfort your child!" I
wasn't saying many words at that point I suppose but I
remember that exact moment, the pattern on the floor,
the drapes, the rocking chair she was nursing the baby in.

Fast forward to myself at between three and four
years old. I was laying in my bed and trying to remember
my conversation with God and what it felt like. I entered
what I now know to be a pseudo-meditative state. I did
go back and re-live this conversation with Him. The
memory of it and the place I went to when I meditated
was identical to the very first time I had memory of it
at all. I have always had this memory. I have never been
without it. It is my gift. I am faithful because faith has

been given to me as a gift. I don't have to wonder about our Creator. I have met Him. I don't have to question where we go when we pass from this world. We go back to where we came from ... heaven ... the universe ... the creation realm, or some version of it. Whatever you want to call it. It is a realm that exists. It is a place without time or space constraints. There are no boundaries. No limitations on what we are, who we are, or where we are.

This experience is a part of my life experience. This is *my* story. It is not limited by any religious belief system. It is just truth. It was and is. It is not to be categorized or boxed into any one view for religion's sake. Religion is a human thing. What I speak of goes before and beyond our human understanding. I have a lot of Christian knowledge and as such, have been given the gift to identify and solidify my experience with affirmations from the Bible. This is not to say that if you share a different religious view that you wouldn't experience the exact same thing. But for the thousands of Christians out there who are searching ... this experience has its roots in scripture.

There is life before our physical bodies are infused with our souls and there is life after our physical bodies die. Our lives are a continuous journey and existence even when we don't have the eyes and ears of our human bodies. Our journey here on earth is a physical one for our spirits, not the other way around. We are spiritual beings having a physical experience. My belief is that everyone here has a purpose, a beautiful intention. We are given the amazing opportunity to experience this world and co-create within it. We are all a perfect reflection of the Creator.

> *Genesis 1:26 Then God said, "Let us make man in our image, after our likeness. And let them have dominion over the fish of the sea and over the birds of the heavens and over the livestock and over all the earth and over every creeping thing that creeps on the earth."*

When God says let *us* make man in *OUR* image, I have always been confused by that. There it is ... *us* and *our*. Growing up in Catholic school, we were taught by the ladies in black that God was lonely so He made man. If God was lonely then why did He say "us and our?" He obviously wasn't alone. My understanding of this after many years of meditation and prayer is that God is actually a *collective* consciousness. We too reflect this multi-faceted consciousness. For instance, we can each be one human entity with numerous roles or facets. We can be mothers, fathers, sisters, brothers, daughters, sons, friends, husbands, wives. Have careers, or be world travelers, be rich, poor, middle class etc. Each one of these roles within the personality are compartmentalized when interacting with others. We tend to emulate one facet of our souls at a time in order to bring what is necessary to a conversation or situation that has presented itself. In the most simple of terms ... you wouldn't speak with a co-worker about your birthing experience in a professional setting or share an intimate relationship detail ... say at the Monday morning meeting.

In order to keep these different aspects of personality ordered, we are still the sum of each aspect but only express ourselves within the parameters and appropriateness of the experience. When we are connected to our divine nature, we emulate all of the aspects of ourselves at once. We radiate our true light within. We are at that moment the essence of true love. I believe that true love is seeing the fullness of another person encompassing all of their true facets of personality and being fascinated to the point that you cannot imagine not having that feeling in your life every day for the rest of your life. Or we can just go with the "Wedding Crasher's" definition...

"True love is your soul's recognition of its counterpoint in another."

CHAPTER 22

LIFE LESSONS

Fulfilling our potential in life is the soul's purpose. We must push through our challenges. Evolve. If we are to become the full expression of the intention of our Creator, it is our purpose to explore, observe, create, love, and embrace our physical realm. Drink it in. Feel its beauty. Listen to the voices of the soul. Look at nature, people, and the creations of human beings as tremendous, amazing, phenomenal potential. Smell the richness of our favorite food, flowers, pumpkin pie, or the familiar aroma of our lover's favorite scent. Just Relax.

Take it all in. This is it! Forget the troubles of today. Yesterday is gone forever and tomorrow is only a promise easily broken by fate. Today is the day to gaze at the moon. Be fascinated by the night sky and its splendor. Close your eyes and allow the warmth of the sun to penetrate your soul. Feel your divine grace as you breathe in your surroundings. Make a careful accounting of those who are in your life. Do they invigorate, encourage, and adore your soul? Do they, even in their human imperfection improve your chances of living your true potential? Are their voices energizing, reassuring, refreshing, and restorative? Or do they dampen, depress, or discourage you? Are they inspiring or frustrating? When you have a conversation do those around you dissuade you from those things you only dream about? Don't hesitate to put space between you and those who thwart your soul efforts. Nothing horrendous is going to happen if you don't have that phone conversation that leaves you feeling damaged, broken, or upset. The world is not going to end if you do not remain friends with that person that you love to hate. When you make the choice to surround yourself with those who uplift you, and care for your soul, your life transforms in a way you never could have imagined while listening to the voices of those who only wanted to keep you in their limited realm of belief.

The choices are yours to freely live whatever expression of yourself you feel moves you closer to being your organic self. Pride and programming are your enemy.

CONCLUSION

The creation realm is real. It is never ending and with no beginning. It is with us all the time. To keep it in perspective, I look at my ancestry. Those thousands of people that came before me to get me here. Those pioneers who set out into uncharted territory, risked their lives and those of their children to blaze a trail of freedom to live. Rode horses, rode in wagons and endured heat, famine and hostiles … those who cooked over open flames. Those who hadn't discovered flame yet! All of those sweet souls have added to my collective existence and are with me every minute of every day wishing the very best for me. They wish for my happiness, peace, understanding and fulfillment. Our ancestors have lived this life and want only our best. They still exist and are connected to us. They carry the wisdom of the ages and are at our beck and call. We can pray them into our lives any time we want if we stay connected to our Creator in a true understanding that we are not alone in this physical existence. We are a sum of everything that has ever been and what is to come. When we leave this world, we become the advisors, the muses, the inspiration for the thoughts of those that are still having this physical experience. We are the light, the faith, the knowledge they seek. We are the Creator and the Creator is us. We have walked the path, finished strong and fulfilled our journey here and we will once again be reunited with our light beings and rejoice in it. We will be the ones that drop pennies from heaven.

For those of us that are struggling, I hope that somehow my experience in the creation realm has inspired you to hold on, push through, ignite your heart with a flame of hope and faith that you are exactly where you are supposed to be, and that things are going to work out for your good.

It has been my experience that those people you interact with here, some of them anyhow, you've met in the creation realm. Like beams of light energy that we effortlessly collided with, we expanded our light experiencing the beauty, power, grace, joy, bliss, intelligence of each other and then passing through and out into the darkness again somehow expanded.

I know I had met Rick in this place. My soul knew it. I knew I had known him before. Never in a physical realm ... only in the Creation realm. He was beautiful to me then and beautiful to me once again when I first set eyes on him. Something inside me recognized him ... I just knew.

My family and his family and friends were forever changed because of his presence here. Our children were born into this realm because of him and we miss his physical touch in our lives daily. But we understand that we were blessed to share him for a time and that all is well. We did not pass from this world. We are still here. We were simply entangled through the heart into his experience and the Creator made him to experience this world for a time and then pass from it. All is well. All is as it should be. We did not pass with him. That was *his* unique life experience. We are not victims of his death, we were so very blessed to share in his life experience here as a physical being and we will again join him in the fullness of his being in the creation realm some call heaven.

But this is also *my* life experience, and my experience is not over. There are still things left for me to say and do, see and observe. I know I had met many of my friends, my children and my love, Roger, there in that blissful realm. It is not my time to leave here, although throughout that cancer journey with my late husband, there were many times I wished it had been me and not him. We cling to this life because we feel *present here.* We feel connected here. We feel loved here. But let me assure you that no other greater or deeper love is there than the peace and connectedness that is felt when we pass from this world to the next. The Creator would not allow us this existence on a whim just to let our lights burn so brightly in the creation realm, then share our light here in this physical place and then just burn out altogether. We are more numerous than the stars. Our light shines brighter than the sun and we are divine, intended, and destined, to be back in this place and share the beauty of this earthly story, with the "others."

And when this life is over here,

I will see those that I have loved and who have loved me while in this physical dance we call being human. I will once again be free of time, space, and physical restraints. I will watch over, protect and inspire those who I've left behind on this physical plane and with my divine inner light shining as brightly as ever continue to love from a place of peace and wisdom.

I will move about effortlessly, recognizing the others, reflecting and appreciating their beauty, grace, knowledge, love and precious being. I will with all my power and might force my light upon them and join in their unending song of existence passing through them effortlessly in a dance of ecstasy. I will once again be home. I will once again be whole... Fulfilled. I will again be reunited with our Creator.

I am Relieved
I am Healed
I am perfect
I am divine
I am potential unleashed
I am limitless
I am Loved
I am Whole

30 CREATION REALM AFFIRMATIONS

- Only when we shine our innermost love and light are we truly organically ourselves.
- It is the true expression of the self that is the real beauty in all of us.
- Focus on those things in life that bring me joy, hope, peace and love and suddenly my life expands with those things.
- Our Creator provides all that we need. We could never run out. Just as the heavens can never run out of stars
- We are never truly alone. All of creation that has come before me is cheering me on to my inner greatness!
- The Creator makes the universe bow down at my feet.
- I am magnificent, intended and loved.
- I have all of the courage I need. It's there in the reservoir of my soul.
- Be happy … it makes other people crazy!
- My life is unfolding exactly as it should. Every experience, even the ones I view as painful or

negative has been divinely inspired and I welcome all new experiences as opportunities for growth.

- My creativity flows constantly. I am creating each moment of my life with grace and ease.
- The purpose of life is joy. There is nothing wrong with achieving joy and wanting and expecting joy for myself and others.
- I am worthy and I am blessed. I am an extension of the Creator and that very Creator is always available to me and flowing through me.
- There are no accidents ... whatever happens to me has been attracted into my experience for a reason.
- Imagine the possibilities of life when we live from our inner light that is limitless.
- Abundance flows easily to me.
- Good things happen to me and for me.
- I am an eternal being whose purpose is to love and live in joy!
- I do not need others to validate me ... I am here because I am valid and I am valid because I am here.
- To truly live to the fullest expression of myself, I must first realize the power that exists in this exact moment. Remembering that today is yesterday's tomorrow and tomorrow's yesterday.

- As of today I do not take offense to the actions of others. I wish for their well-being instead, as a fellow being of light, love and intention.
- Feeling vulnerable is a state of mind and is NOT a threat to my wellness as an individual.
- I refuse to limit myself because others need to define me due to their lack of understanding my full potential.
- I begin each day with gratefulness. I put my feet on the floor and lift my hands to the sky and thank the Creator for the day and the opportunities it brings.
- I am grateful for those who surround me and especially those that bring me joy.
- I am present in each moment. I appreciate nature, and the beauty that surrounds me each day.
- No matter where I am or what I am going through, I can and will make it.
- I will do three things each day that move me closer to the person I was born to be.
- I enjoy the process of "getting there." For in between where I am and where I want to be is my life.
- Today IS the day

This is the end of the book, however, it's never THE END …

We are infinite beings and our light shines on forever…

It shines as brightly now as it did before you were YOU!

Printed in the United States
By Bookmasters